The 88

This script is published by
DCG Publications.

All inquiries regarding purchase of further scripts and current royalty rates should be addressed to:

DCG Media Group
Vamos 73008
Chania
Crete
Greece

Email: info@dcgmediagroup.com
www.dcgmediagroup.com

Conditions

- ❖ All DCG Publication scripts are fully protected by the copyright acts. Under no circumstances must they be reproduced by photo-copying or any other means, either in whole or in part.

- ❖ The license to perform referred to above only relates to live performances of this script. A separate license is required for video-taping or sound recording, which will be issued on receipt of the appropriate fee.

- ❖ The name of the author shall be clearly stated on all publicity, programs etc. The program credits shall state "Script provided by DCG Publications".

The 88

By

Glyn Jones

DCG
Publications

First Published in Greece 2010

© Glyn Idris Jones
The author's moral rights have been asserted

DCG Publications
www.dcgmediagroup.com

ISBN 978-960-98418-5-6

Typeset by
DCG Publications

Printed in England by
Lightning Source.

First Produced
at the

Old Vic Theatre Company,
November 1979

Directed by
Christopher Selbie

Design
Bob Crowley

Lighting
Bill Wardroper

Cast List

Keith Bartlett	Pvt. Oliver / Sgt. Shaw
Steven Beard	Pvt. Egan
Roger Blake	Pvt. Sweeney
Colin Bruce	Pvt. Sears
Mark Buffery	Pvt. James Daly
Ray Callaghan	Pvt. Gleeson
Nick Garden	Soldier in firing party
John Gording	Pvt. Joseph Hawes
Micheal Gardiner	Pvt. Gogarty / Prison Guard
Richard Harradine	Pvt. Lally / Second Guard
Art Malik	The Nappi / Sentry / Sergeant
Trevor Martin	Col. Jackson / Father Baker
Ralph Michael	Col. Deacon
Rob Middleton	Pvt. Hynes / First Guard
Robert Putt	Pvt. Fitzgerald
Ronnie Stevens	Maj. Lloyd
Hugh Sullivan	Maj. Alexander
Paul Toothill	Maj. Payne / Lt Smythe Officer in charge of firing party
Janet Maw	Voice of James Daly's mother

Members of the cast with Christopher Selbie (Director) & Glyn Jones (author)
THE 88 - Old Vic Theatre Company - November 1979

Photograph by Christopher Davies

One special hero in our midst, James Daly was his name,
And manfully he stood his trial and thought his crime no shame.
The court they found him guilty and Sydney Lawford then did say,
The 2nd of November, lad, will be your dying day.
Twelve of Daly's comrades also condemned to die
Were pardoned all while waiting in the prison of Dagshai.
But Daly's pardon never came, tho' expected one afternoon,
And at eight o'clock the following morn this lad went to his doom.
He was like a living angel when walking out to die
This gallant Irish martyr, no tear did dim is eye,
Althou' he died in Dagshai jail twas for a noble deed,
So I hope you'll pray for Daly in the county of Westmeath.
And now our trial is over and our punishment it starts,
Altho' it's penal servitude it won't break our Irish hearts;
And if Ireland gets her freedom, some day we my go home,
But I'll never forget the eighty-eight they call "The Devil's Own."

> From a poem written in Dagshai Prison
> by "40" Walsh, Connaught Rangers

The men acted only as they did because of what was happening in Ireland and because they believed they were fighting for the rights of small nations.

> From a letter to the Irish Defence Journal, Vol XIX No 4 Nov 1959 from Frank W. Keenan Corporal 32400 Connaught Rangers.

The Connaught Rangers was founded in 1793 by the Earl of Clanricarde and took part in almost every campaign undertaken by the British army in the Peninsular and Crimea, Boer War, World War I and Palestine as the 88th of the Line. The number of mutineers brought to trial was 88.

CAST

(In order of appearance)

PRIVATE JAMES DALY
1ST GUNNER
2ND GUNNER
FATHER BAKER
MAJOR LLOYD
PRIVATES HAWES
        SWEENY
        GOGARTY
        LALLY
COLONEL DEACON
COLONEL JACKSON
THE NAPPI
PRIVATES GLEESON
        SEARS
        FITZGERALD
        EGAN
        OLIVER
MAJOR ALEXANDER
PRIVATE HYNES
SENTRY
DALY'S MOTHER (Voice off)
MAJOR PAYNE
SOUTH WALES BORDERERS
LIEUTENANT
LIEUTENANT SMYTH
SERGEANT
LIEUTENANT IN CHARGE OF FIRING PARTY
ESCORT

Act One

India 2nd November, 1920. There is the sound of men's voices singing an Irish rebel song, "Will My Soul Pass Over Ireland?" As a pool of light fades in on a cell in the Military prison at Dagshai a bugle sounds reveille and the singing abruptly stops. We see a plain whitewashed wall crudely decorated with prisoner's drawings: shamrocks, a crucifix, a hangman's noose, the regimental badge of the Connaught Rangers consisting of harp and scroll and, written large, "The 88th."

Outside the cell there stands on trestles a traitor's coffin that is painted black and white stripes. The lid is off and leaning against it.

A figure seated on the floor, his back to the wall, arms folded across his knees, lifts his head. This is PRIVATE JAMES DALY.

Also in the cell are two GUNNERS seated on a bench. They look up as DALY moves, wipes the tension from his face with both hands and then, getting to his feet, stands in such a position that, looking through the grille in the door, were it there in actuality, he can see the coffin.

DALY   Sweet Jesus, does it not give a man a strange feeling to see it standing there? *(He laughs)* And it's a poor bed for an Irish martyr to be spending eternity in. Well... no more than is fitting and proper for a private soldier I suppose and once it's under the sod no one will see the colour of it. It is a real coffin at least which is more than a lot of poor bastards get. Do you fancy meeting your maker wrapped in an army blanket? Give the British army its due. The military may be a wee bit on the simple side but it knows the place for everything and everything in its place. *(Coming to attention)* One Irish rebel all present and correct, sir. One Irish dog, sir. One scapegoat, sir. One execution for the example of... sah! *(His hand goes to his mouth as he verges on*

1

breaking) Holy Mother of God! It's me that I'm talking about. It's now that I'm talking about. The here and now... that I'm talking about.

He pulls himself together and turns to smile at the GUNNERS one of whom is very young and has risen on his hands from the bench.

DALY   Sit down, son. Sit down. Don't you know the Irish are the greatest talkers on God's earth? Earth? It's the hosts of Gods heaven I'll soon be driving mad with my gabbling. God bless the Irish. Tellers of tales and spinners of moonbeams. Every good, patriotic Englishman knows that. The same as he knows we grow spuds when we can and our cottages make lovely bonfires, that we're Papists, and we spend our days and nights singing and getting drunk, and believe in the little people and there's a crock of gold at the end of every rainbow. In a word, gunner we are not so much people of flesh and blood as a mixture of peat bog, bullshit and fairytales. I wonder what it's like to be shot. Ah well, at least it will be quick. That's if they don't all get the bloody jitters. Fancy me then, Saint Sebastian Daly... Saint James Daly of Tyrrel's Pass in the County of Westmeath. When they were bringing us here, after the sentence, do you know I passed that nappi... what did he come here for?... all the way from Solon... that poor skinny little black bastard I've kicked up the arse so often my foot hurt. And he was crying do you know that? Standing there in the sun and sand with tears streaming down the dust of his face and snot running from his nose and the flies feeding off his sweat. I saw him there "Sewer ki bacha" I called him and he burst out howling like his own child had died. Do you think he'll shave me when I'm dead? They say hair grows a while after. For a while after. They're taking their bloody time about it aren't they?

There is the sound of jangling keys, a moment, then a bolt is slammed back and FATHER BAKER enters the pool of light. He looks at the GUNNERS who rise and go. The younger one pauses, turns, goes back slowly to DALY. Silently he holds out his hand. DALY does not take the hand but places his own on the boy's shoulder gives it a little shake and then turns away. The boy goes.

BAKER   How are you then, Jimmy?

DALY   As well as might be expected, Father, considering all the circumstances.

BAKER   You don't change.

DALY   There wouldn't seem to be much point in changing now would there?

BAKER: Would there not?

He permits himself a slight smile in answer to DALY's, then seats himself on the bench and, placing his elbow on his knee, holds his open hand against his face. For a moment DALY does not move. FATHER BAKER looks up.

DALY   I was just thinking, Father, there's not been all that opportunity for sinning lately.

BAKER   While you are still in your earthly body sin is with you, even in this bare cell.

DALY   Hmn... you might be right at that.

DALY goes down on his knees beside the priest who resumes his original position and waits as DALY lifts his left knee and brushes it off.

                A stone. Right on my scar. It was hurting.

BAKER   Ready?

DALY nods.

                    Dominus sit in corde tuo et in labilis tuis. In nominé Patris et Filii et Spiritus Sancti, Amen.

DALY   I confess to Almighty God, to Blessed Mary ever a virgin. To Blessed Michael the Archangel, Blessed John the Baptist, to the Holy Apostles, Peter and Paul. To all the Saints, and to you, Father, that I have sinned exceedingly in thought, word, and deed through my fault, through my fault, through my most grievous fault.

As DALY recites the above the lights come up on a general field court martial. At a long central table sits GENERAL SIR SYDNEY LAWFORD presiding and flanked by three officers on either side, captains and majors. In front of the long table sits MAJOR TUCKER, the Judge Advocate. These figures can all be seated in shadow or silhouette. They could even be cardboard cut-outs. The man we are concerned with is to the right and at right angles to the central table. This is MAJOR LLOYD, Prosecuting Council and himself of the Connaughts. The witness table is on Major Tucker's left and directly facing him would be the prisoners with armed escort on either side, but these we do not see.

                3 Officers. General Lawford. 3 Officers.

                      Major Tucker.
                      Witness Table.
                      Major Lloyd.

                Escort. Prisoners. Escort.

LLOYD   Mr President, may it please the court, the contention of the Crown is that, on the morning of Monday, June 28th, 1920, the men of B Company, D Company, and a detachment of C Company, The Connaught Rangers, stationed at Wellington Barracks, Jullundur, despite all arguments and appeals from their officer for a return to duty, refused to parade and served on their officer the following notice which I read to the court.

PRIVATE JOSEPH HAWES enters downstage where he can directly address the audience.

HAWES   I bring to your notice the recent troubles committed by British troops in Ireland. The Connaught Rangers are determined to stand by Sinn Fein. Our indignation will be shown by acts and not words. We cannot stand by as Irish men and see our relatives murdered. We demand the withdrawal of the military from Ireland.

LLOYD   You will hear, gentlemen, of how mutiny stemmed directly from the word and actions of...

HAWES   The British in Ireland.

LLOYD   ...four men, Privates Sweeny, Gogarty, Lally and Hawes.

During the above the cell has been struck and a table placed by the bench with more seating (bench or stools) as necessary. As each man's name is mentioned he appears on stage and finally HAWES, on his own name, crosses over to the group.

HAWES   Have youse had any news from home?

They shake their heads.

GOGARTY   Who would want any? News from home is bad news.

SWEENY   It doesn't want thinking about.

LALLY   True. I could do with a beer.

He gives GOGARTY a hard look. GOGARTY, who has a bottle in his hand, ignores it.

HAWES   Sometimes I take a look at myself...

GOGARTY   That's bad news.

HAWES   And I say to myself, what is to become of you, Joseph Hawes, I says, playing at being a soldier boy for the King of England?

SWEENY   Soldiers? In France we was soldiers. Here we're policemen. Bloody police, that's all we are.

GOGARTY   What else? *(He takes a drink).*

LALLY   I could do with a beer, but I got no more credit. Bloody Punjabis.

SWEENY   There's no good reason for them to be doing you any favours, Stephen Lally.

GOGARTY   How was it when you were home, Josie?

HAWES   What do you want me to tell you? It was all roses? Sometimes I wonder what it is I'm doing here at all. I'll tell you. Did youse know that all assemblies in County Clare is proclaimed? Well now, would you be calling a hurling match an assembly?

GOGARTY   If you was playing maybe I would.

LALLY   I don't know. Would you?

HAWES   The British call it that. A hurling match! Is that a political thing?

LALLY   I don't know. Is it?

HAWES   Well this hurling match I saw with my own eyes broken up by troops.

LALLY   Is that right now?

HAWES   With bayonets.

LALLY   The bastards!

HAWES   At the point of their bloody toothpicks and that's a fact as I'm standing here.

SWEENY   I've had a letter.

GOGARTY   Moran's had a letter too. He showed it to me. And the newspapers. I've seen them. Some terrible things is going on.

HAWES   Do you know what I think? I think that what we're doing here is no more than what the British forces is doing in Ireland and that's a fact.

SWEENY   What are we going to do about it then?

LALLY   *(Startled)* Us?

SWEENY   Yes. We should do something.

LALLY   I could do with a beer. A cup of char even.

SWEENY   We should make a protest.

GOGARTY   Words is cheap.

SWEENY   We should make a protest.

HAWES   Paddy's right.

LLOYD   These men must be held responsible, even if

indirectly, for all that followed.

The MEN have left the table and now stand in front of it.

LLOYD   You will hear evidence from Sergeant Shaw, guard sergeant at Jullundur on the morning of the 28th.

SERGEANT SHAW has entered and seats himself at the table. He looks up at the men in front of him.

SHAW   What are you men doing here?

HAWES   As a protest against British atrocities in Ireland we refuse to soldier any longer in the service of the king. Lock us up.

For a moment SHAW stares at them. Then he laughs.

GOGARTY   And what are ye laughing at?

SHAW   No, I shouldn't be laughing, that's the truth. It's too early in the morning for jokes and oh, my God, it's hot and will you all get the bloody hell out of here before I take you serious like?

LALLY   That's it.

SHAW   That's what?

LALLY   Take us serious. Because we mean it.

SHAW   *(Looks from one to the other and then roars)* Gerrout of here!

SWEENY   No. We want to be locked up.

SHAW   You do, you do, but not in one of my cells. It's a padded cell you'd be wanting. Holy Mother of God have you all gone stark raving mad? It's the heat. That's what it is. It's the heat that gets

|||youse. See the M.O. Lie down. Take it easy. Ye'll be all right in a day or so.

HAWES   *(Quietly)* Lock us up.

SHAW   You're trying to make a monkey out of me!

GOGARTY   No.

SHAW   And what am I to say when I report this? *(Smacking a hand down on his stripes)* Do you want me to lose these? Now, for the last time, will you please go away?

No one moves. SHAW looks appealingly from one to the other.

All right then, you asked for it. Squad, squad shun! Right turn! By the left, quick march!

GOGARTY, LALLY and SWEENY go.

Pick 'em up there! Left right left right!

He follows them out.

HAWES   Would you not have given the whole British Empire to see his face then? About an hour later it must have been he got another shock when C Company paraded. Private Moran he steps out of the ranks and...

LLOYD   This man publicly addressed his sergeant, saying...

HAWES   "I refuse to parade and I want to be put in the guardroom with the other four men who are gone there in Ireland's cause."

LLOYD   You will hear how the sergeant ordered two men, Corporal Cox and Lance Corporal Keenan

	to place Moran in the guardroom.
HAWES	Easier said than done. Cox and Keenan weren't having any. "We are in sympathy with the men in the guardroom" they said, so in they went too. And were they not followed by twenty-nine men of C Company and their duty guard who threw down his rifle and brought up the rear? Closing the gate behind him as polite as you please.
LLOYD	You will hear evidence from Lance Corporal John Flannery who was in the affair from the beginning.
HAWES	When it started do you see we gave Lance Corporal Flannery who was a pal of Lally's our home addresses in case we were shot out of hand. Then he could write to our people and tell 'em what really happened. The bastard later tried to turn king's evidence. Said he only did what he did to keep the officers informed, in touch with what was going on.

As he talks, HAWES passes off the table and benches and now there is an off-stage cacophony; snatches of rebel songs and a continuous chant of "Up the Republic! Up the Republic!" The noise is deafening. During it, COLONEL DEACON takes his place at the witness table and, the noise dying down, LLOYD acknowledges him.

LLOYD	And you will hear from Colonel Deacon, officer commanding, how word of the mutiny spread. *(He turns to DEACON).* B Company had just returned from the rifle range, is that right, sir?
DEACON	Correct. There was this unholy noise coming from the guardroom and when I, together with the adjutant and Regimental Sergeant Major Tame came on the scene B Company had halted about eighty yards away so I told them to wait on

	the steps of a bungalow nearby while I discussed the matter with the men in the guardroom. I ordered the duty sergeant to release them so that I could address them outside.
HAWES	That's right. We came out and fell in in single rank facing him. He started off by telling us of his own service in the Connaughts, thirty-three years of it.
DEACON	I reminded the men of the great and proud history of the Connaught Rangers and drew attention to the honours on our battle flag.
HAWES	He did that.
DEACON	*(Turning to face HAWES)* I point out to you that, as the 88th of the Line, this regiment has taken part in almost every campaign undertaken by the British army in the Peninsular and Crimea, the Boer War, World War, yes, and in Palestine. Must I remind you of how we won our great fighting reputation at Scringapatam? Under Wellington at Salamanca and Badajoz? How we gallantly upheld it at Colenso and Pieter's Hill? And, as part of the 10th Irish Division, did we not fight with distinction in the Dardanelles and then in Serbia? We captured the Kabak Kuyu wells and the Kaiajak Aghala near Anzac, two of the proudest achievements in the history of our great fighting regiment.
LLOYD	The men listened to you?
DEACON	What man could fail to feel the stirrings of patriotism when reminded of such a record? I then advised them to return to their bungalows and the whole unfortunate incident would be decently forgotten.
LLOYD	And how did they react to this - how shall I put

	it - generous offer?
HAWES	Well he had me worried for one. He had tears in his eyes as he spoke and that's a fact.
DEACON	At first the men responded very well until private Hawes took it upon himself to step forward and say...
HAWES	*(Stepping forward)* All the honours on the Connaught flag are for England, there are none for Ireland, but there is going to be one today and it is going to be the greatest honour of them all.
LLOYD	A stirring reply.
HAWES	Which was just what it was meant to be.
LLOYD	What happened then, sir?
DEACON	The adjutant turned to Regimental Sergeant Major Tame and said, when the men went back to their bungalows to put Hawes back under arrest, but one of the men...
HAWES	Coman it was, further down the line, private Coman from Tipperary, he said...
DEACON	"You won't get the chance of Hawes, we're all going back".
HAWES	Then he shouted, "Left turn, back to the guardroom, lads." So we all went back and got ourselves locked up again.
DEACON	I, and the other officers, then returned to the B Company men who had been watching and listening to all this, and ordered them back to their bungalows. But most of them refused and, I'd say about a hundred, went over to the

guardhouse and started talking to the others through the bars. The B Company men were still armed of course and they ordered the duty sergeant to open the guardroom door, which he did.

HAWES So we all trooped out again and had a little parley when we decided to hold a meeting in the regimental theatre.

DEACON *(Almost to himself)* A mutiny was unthinkable. Unthinkable. What! On the very doorstep of British Army H.Q.? In the centre of a Sikh stronghold?

LLOYD *(Consulting papers)* You then saw the men...

DEACON What? Oh, yes. Later in the afternoon. They arrived at my quarters and demanded an interview. It seems they had elected a committee of seven men to act on behalf of the general body.

LLOYD These men were... *(Reading)* Privates Sweeny, Gogarty, Moran, Hawes, Lance Corporals McGowan and Flannery, and Corporal James Davis.

DEACON They had elected a spokesman, Lance Corporal Flannery.

HAWES The bastard.

DEACON And they drew up some orders.

HAWES Some? Some? I'll tell you. What we decided at this committee meeting then is that our aim should be to make an open protest to the whole world about what the British are doing in Ireland. But order must be kept in barracks with the same discipline as though the officers

	was still in charge.
LLOYD	I have here the orders drawn up by the committee.
HAWES	*(Taking paper from his pocket)* One, that all men retain their arms. Two, to change the guard and replace it with a double guard of our own. Three, to put a sentry on guard at each of the two canteens, wet and dry. I reckon that to be very necessary.
LLOYD	Four, that the Union Jack on the flagstaff be replaced by the Irish flag.
HAWES	*(Looking up over his paper and grimacing)* That really hurt. *(He returns to his paper)* Five, to put on flying sentries at night and special patrols. Six, to separate the mutineers from the men who remain loyal to the king and to give the loyal men protection.
LLOYD	And what, sir, was your reply to all this?
DEACON	I told them I was particularly worried about the natives. I thought, if there was any chance at all of them getting at the arms, they might attack our men. I reminded them of the troubled times, the unrest, particularly with that fellow Ghandi going around stirring up trouble, and with the army having to be called out at all times to reinforce the police.
LLOYD	And what was the response to that?
DEACON	It was Hawes again, always Hawes. He replied...
HAWES	If I am to be shot I rather it was an Indian would shoot me than an Englishman.
LLOYD	How would you describe Hawes' manner

	towards you, sir?
DEACON	What?
LLOYD	Would you say it was - insolent?
DEACON	What would you call it?
LLOYD	According to the summary of evidence taken in July/August, the adjutant states that Hawes behaved in an extremely disrespectful manner towards you, even so far as to be smoking a cigarette while speaking.
HAWES	Well, apart from the smoking of a cigarette which I was not, nothing else important happened that day that I know of, or that night. Not in the barracks anyway, though there was rumours, there's always rumours.
LLOYD	On the morning of the twenty-ninth, Colonel Jackson, representing General Munroe, C-In-C British forces in India, arrived at the barracks in Jullundur.
HAWES	He drove up with a white flag on his car. The sentries allowed him in to the orderly room where he asked if he could meet the committee.

COLONEL DEACON having retired, his place is now taken by JACKSON. HAWES takes from his pocket a tricolour which he pins to his tunic and turns to face JACKSON though he still addresses his asides to the audience.

| JACKSON | Men... *(He clears his throat)* I am here as the representative of General Munroe. Perhaps he sent me because, being meself a Roscommon man, I am not afraid to come into your barracks, hey? As you can see, I know the honour of the Irish. I know you for what you are, all honourable men. |

HAWES   Do you know I had the feeling he was quoting from something, but not being a literary man meself I wasn't too sure.

JACKSON   And, believe me, I also appreciate the qualities of the Irishman as a fighter. Doesn't everyone in the British army?

HAWES   Don't they just?

JACKSON   In particular I know the calibre of the Connaught Rangers. However... however... the fact is, no matter how good you are as soldiers, among the best, no doubt of that, your barracks will have to be taken and occupied by loyal troops. Have to. Even if it takes every last soldier in India to do so.

HAWES   And what I wonder will the restless natives be up to while all this jolly old shenanigan is going on?

JACKSON   Overcome ye'll be, make no mistake about it, and I must point out to you that, if it comes to a clash, there will be the most serious loss of life. *(He looks around as though surveying a whole line of men)* Who amongst you will be prepared to accept responsibility for that? Face the dreadful consequences? Any of you?

HAWES   If we be still alive do ye mean?

JACKSON   I might also point out to you that you are in a strange land many miles from home.

HAWES   Sure now and there's no need to remind us of that.

JACKSON   If you did break out, where would you go? What would you do? You are surrounded by

	hostile elements.
HAWES	And there's no need to remind us of that either.
JACKSON	However, there is no question of your breaking out. There is no retreat for any of you. You are already encircled.
HAWES	True enough. Even the artillery they had brought up.
JACKSON	My mission then is to offer you the opportunity now to surrender your arms and to tell you that the authorities will forward your complaints in the proper manner to the proper quarters where they will be fairly considered.
HAWES	And what be your fair and proper terms, sir?
JACKSON	Yes... *(He clears his throat)* Firstly that a party of British troops will enter your barracks and disarm you. You will then proceed to a camp on the plains which will be specially prepared for you. There you will wait for an answer to your protests.
HAWES	No, sir. Begging your pardon, sir, them be not proper terms at all, sir. If anybody is to collect the arms it will be us who will be doing it. And it will be our own who will be guarding them. After that we will march to your special camp, sir, but proudly under our own committee and not a British soldier in sight.
JACKSON	No, I cannot agree to that.
HAWES	Then, sir, a fight it must be, to the bitter end, sir. And, by the Sacred Name, I mean that.

There is a long pause as the two men face each other, then LLOYD step forward.

LLOYD   The discussion continued until the evening with Colonel Jackson in constant touch with headquarters by telephone but it was finally agreed on the mutineers' terms and the surrender was arranged to take place on the evening of July the first.

JACKSON and LLOYD leave the stage.

HAWES   It was the day in between as it were. We were all busy cleaning and stacking our arms in a bungalow when Keenan and Kelly, they came up to me and suggested they might slip away to Solon up in the hills and tell the lads there, the rest of C Company that is, what it was that was going on. Well, it was worth a try. With a little wit and luck they might get through.

HAWES leaves the stage.

The 1st July, 1920. A barrack room, Solon. The room would hold twenty beds or so. We see a corner of it and five beds, those of PRIVATES DALY, GLEESON, SEARS, FITZGERALD AND EGAN. The scene is of the utmost simplicity. At the foot of each bed is a kit box on top of which stands a washing bowl upside down. On the wall at the head of each bed hangs the occupant's kit: a haversack, belt and pouches, water bottle upside down, mess tin. A door leads out on to the verandah, part of which can be seen. It is dark, the darkness just before dawn, and the men are asleep.

A LIGHT appears on the verandah and a second or two later a figure enters the room. It is the NAPPI. He carries a hurricane lamp; cracked, soot-blackened glass: a small bowl of water; a dirty, torn towel, shaving brush and cut-throat razor. (Note: The men would normally be sleeping under mosquito nets but, as this is Solon in the hills and for the sake of simplicity in production, I think they can be dispensed with though they may be used if wanted.) The NAPPI approaches the nearest bed which is DALY's. He places the lamp on the floor and turns the sleeping man's head into a position for lathering. He has no sooner applied the second stroke of the brush when DALY, yelling blue murder, leaps from the bed. The startled NAPPI jumps back and the other men wake up. DALY is now sitting on his bed, feeling his face and examining his fingers for signs of blood. There is a general moan of "What the bloody hell?" "What's on?" "It's Daly again." etc. The petrified NAPPI, still holding the brush, is standing between the beds gazing in horror at DALY who now turns to survey him. Without a word, DALY climbs off the bed and, in silence, slowly approaches the NAPPI who, at the last second, makes a desperate dive for the door, is grabbed by DALY and hurled back between the beds.

DALY	Sewer ki bacha! I tell you it's me throat he's after cutting. He's been trying to cut me throat ever since we got here.

He tests his cheek again for signs of blood.

EGAN	It's a funny place you keep your throat.
DALY	*(Turning back to the Nappi)* Isn't that right?
NAPPI	*(Shaking his head vigorously)* No, please!
DALY	Come here.
NAPPI	No please.
DALY	I'm going to kick your arse for you. What am I going to do, nappi?
NAPPI	Kick my arse for me please.
DALY	Come here then.

DALY points to the floor in front of him. The NAPPI stands still and shakes his head again.

GLEESON	Oh, shut up, Daly, for God's sake and let us get

	some sleep.
DALY	Sleep? Sleep? By all the saints how can I sleep when I've just been sliced open from ear to ear? I tell you. There's not a single mother's son of these bastards you can trust. No, nor their mothers neither.
SEARS	You shouldn't say things like that about anybody's mother. No, not even black ones. You wouldn't like it, someone saying things like that about your mother.
DALY	Come here, nappi. You can't get out so you might as well.

Gingerly the NAPPI approaches DALY and cringes in front of him.

| GLEESON | Ah, leave him alone, Jimmy. |
| DALY | Now by all the saints what would you be wanting to do a thing like that to me for, hmn? |

The NAPPI grins broadly. Suddenly DALY grabs him by the shirt and pulls the man towards him.

Now give me that thing.

With his free hand he grabs the brush, feels it, then lifts it up for all to see before tossing it to GLEESON.

DALY	Look at that will youse! Didn't I tell you? Three hog's hairs and a bloody great six inch nail!
GLEESON	It's a tack. A tiny little wee tin tack.
DALY	It's a nail, you idiot. Are you blind?
GLEESON	To the whole world I was, not five minutes ago if you hadn't opened your big mouth. Well,

	now that I am well and truly awake, he might just as well be getting on with me. You wouldn't want him to be lathering you with a six inch nail now, would you?
DALY	Four annas a week I pay him just to have my throat cut.
FITZGERALD	Four annas a week we all pay him.
EGAN	And if he doesn't get on with cutting your throat pretty damn soon we'll have to stop paying him.

They all laugh. The NAPPI grins but not towards DALY. GLEESON has sat on a kit box and, having soaped the brush, the NAPPI lifts it towards his cheek. Gently GLEESON pushes the hand away.

GLEESON	Not with that, nappi boy, use your hand.
EGAN	He's supposed to be shaving you, Gleeson, not...
NAPPI	Yes, sir, at once, immediately, sir.

He starts to rub soap into GLEESON's cheek. One of the men starts singing very quietly. DALY, leaning against the doorpost, turns to look outside.

DALY	God, it's hot. Hot. It's going to be a scorcher and the sun not even showing his face yet.
FITZGERALD	*(Sniffing his armpits)* Sure I'm sweating like a pig.
SEARS	*(Giggling)* That's because you are a pig.
FITZGERALD	Only for sharing your sty.
DALY	*(Turns to look back into the room and laughs)* Sears, I've told you before haven't I? You're too young to take on veterans.

21

FITZGERALD	He's too young to take on anything, aren't you, baby?
SEARS	I am not a baby.
EGAN	His mouth not dry from the tit yet.
GLEESON	Jesus Christ! Will youse take a look at that now?

He is holding up the NAPPI's hand in which is the razor. The NAPPI grins uncomfortably around the room.

If that hasn't more ups and downs than the hills of Killarney. *(Gently)* Go away. Go away. Gather up your things and do an alley before you gets a toothpick up youse.

The NAPPI passes in front of GLEESON to collect his basin etc.

God, he stinks of curry. How can anybody stink of curry at five o'clock in the morning?

FITZGERALD	It comes out of his pores. He sweats it out.
GLEESON	Have you got your things?
NAPPI	Yes, sir. Yes, sir. I got them.
GLEESON	Then piss off will ye.

The NAPPI starts to go. They suddenly all yell at him rather like chasing off an unwanted dog and the NAPPI streaks for the door where DALY grabs him.

DALY	And this evening when you come back you will have a new brush, yes?
NAPPI	Yes, sir. Brand spanking new, sir.

GLEESON   And a new razor, yes?

NAPPI   Oh yes, at once, immediately, sir.

DALY   Right.

He propels the NAPPI through the door.

GLEESON   So much for being shaved this morning.

It is lighter now and there is a moment of complete stillness before GLEESON moves.

                Shall we get ready then? *(He gets a towel to take the soap from his face).*

DALY   It's too hot to move.

FITZGERALD   That's the truth.

GLEESON   I'm thinking these two days past must have been the hottest since we got here.

EGAN   I think I'll attend sick parade this morning.

FITZGERALD   No, I wouldn't do that.

EGAN   Why not?

FITZGERALD   You'll get that wee umbrella thing up youse and you wouldn't like that.

SEARS   What umbrella thing?

EGAN   Ah, why did they ever have to send us to India? Black women will be the death of me so they will.

GLEESON   All women will be the death of you, John Egan, and that's a fact.

The men start getting dressed.

EGAN The women are always after me. Sure I don't know why. But it's the black ones'll destroy me.

SEARS Were you ever married, Egan?

EGAN I was a little bit married once, but not much. Ah this terrible country. The blackness of it will be the death of me.

SEARS I like it here.

They all turn to look at him.

SEARS In Solon I mean.

GLEESON Did I not tell you? A baby.

SEARS It's better than Jullundur at least.

GLEESON That's true. There's always others worse off than yourself. *(As an afterthought)* If youse were to look hard enough.

EGAN No, it's true, by God, the lad's right. Jullundur's a stinking hole. I think maybe God had a bit of an off day when he made that place.

GLEESON I think God had a bit of an off day when he made you.

FITZGERALD There's a cinema there at least.

GLEESON That pit? The fleas jump twenty five feet in that place. I tell you they hold the world jumping record those fleas in there.

FITZGERALD True the pictures is always old.

GLEESON And always breaking down, every five minutes,

	just like me old woman.
EGAN	Who goes to see the pictures?
GLEESON	That's right. Everyone goes to see you making an amadain of yourself.
EGAN	Sure I did in the bullring one night there. Did I never tell youse that? Ten bob was all I had in the world. And there she was. Wait till I tell you. I chose the little thing for meself. She was young. She was white. She was everywhere. Ten shillings I had and I never knew where I was. Got me legs around me neck and damn near choking me and me ten bob gone. I was a fool to give it to her first. Didn't know whether I was there or not I can tell you. It'll be the death of me this country. Don't know why I ever joined the army. What do I get out of it but the knocks.
FITZGERALD	You don't even get those by the sound of it.
EGAN	Women is my hobby. Can I help that? I'd embrace them all if I could so help me. Did I never tell you about Biddy McCann? Wait till I tell you. "Here I am," says she, "I can fuck, fight, chaw tobacco, and play the melodeon all at once." And by God she could too.
SEARS	It's a bit cooler here at least. And the hills is very pretty.

They all turn to look at him again. This is hardly a soldier's remark.

	Well are they not? Irish hills almost.
DALY	There's no hills where I come from. It's all flat.
EGAN	Why do they call it a pass then? If it's a pass then it's a pass between something isn't it? It

can't be a pass between nothing, between flat. Are youse listening to me? *(Ignored, he tries again)* Has nobody got a fag? *(Still no response)* Someone tell me, why did I ever join this bloody army? Next thing it'll be ceremonial guard at the bloody Viceroy's. Torture that is. Sheer bloody torture. About all you can move is your eyeballs.

GLEESON   Makes a change for you that does.

EGAN   Not that even that's allowed. This is no bloody army for a man.

SEARS   We're lucky to be in it to my way of thinking.

FITZGERALD   That's true, Vice Regal Hall and all. There's plenty empty bellies and idle hands back home ready, willing, and able to take the king's shilling and our places. And put up with it - heat, crabs, fleas, flies, stink, holy cows, shit and all.

EGAN   Not forgetting the clap, the dhobi's itch and the prickly heat. Empty belly or not its back home I'd like to be right this instant. Don't tell me the grub in the British army is all that warming to the stomach. Stew stew stew, nothing but stew, and not even a good Irish stew at that but a poor English slop.

FITZGERALD   It's regular.

SEARS   And you can always get a crumb-chop from the charwallah.

EGAN   *(Pulls a wry face)* Do you know where I'd like to be? I'd like this moment to be walking down Sackville Street with a girl on my arm.

FITZGERALD   Is that where she'd be?

GLEESON	Not much he could do in the middle of Sackville Street now is there? She'd have to be safe if they was walking.
FITZGERALD	I wouldn't trust him with any girl I know, no, not even in broad daylight walking down Sackville Street.
EGAN	Is it my fault the women all run after me?
GLEESON	One of these days, my bucko, some nasty Hindu gentleman is going to take it into his head to spear you right in the knackers and that'll be the Lord's punishment for your lechery.
FITZGERALD	On the other hand maybe he's all gab.
SEARS	Well we shouldn't talk like that about women anyways. It's disrespectful.
EGAN	And tell me what's disrespectful about it. Was it not the mother of us all who tempted the first man into sinning? And where would you all not be if it hadn't been for that?
SEARS	That's blasphemy!
GLEESON	Now, lads, now... I know the heat is something terrible to bear but let's not be having too much of it between ourselves. Poor old Ireland if we have to fight each other.

DALY turns back from the door.

DALY	No. Not poor Ireland. Never poor Ireland. When I was a little lad back home, my teacher, Nora Feehan, God bless her, she taught me a little song that I was always singing. Working or playing everyone in Tyrell's Pass they would always hear me singing.

FITZGERALD   Hadn't ye better get ready, Jim?

DALY   *(Singing)* She is a rich and rare land
               Oh, she's a fresh and fair land,
               I'd freely die to save her,
               And think my lot divine.

GLEESON   The thing is, Jim, 'tis not for Ireland we'll be dyin' but for England.

FITZGERALD   It's English money that pays us. Its English money we send back home.

EGAN   And it's English money keeps the English in Ireland and their soldiers stealing our women while we have to be doing the best we can with black ones that will be the death of me.

DALY   My father, he was a county Mayo man, a baker by trade, he was in the British army. And my two brothers, John and Paddy. They both died from fighting in France. 'Tis a funny thing you know but the English are never grateful for their friends. Well, God rest them, they died in Ireland at least. Trench fever it was killed off my brother John. He was set in the house looking over the country and suddenly he looks up at the mother and he says, "Mother, ye've never refused me anything, get me just one breath of air." Then he died.

FITZGERALD   Hadn't ye better get ready, Jim?

DALY   *(Nods)* It was for England he died but, when I go, it will be for Ireland. *(He sings softly as he starts to get dressed)*

               She is a rich and rare land,
               Oh, she's a fresh and fair land,
               I'd freely die to save her,
               And think my lot divine.

The LIGHTS go down on the bungalow and come up on the court martial. LLOYD is sorting through his papers. Having done this he turns and steps forward.

LLOYD   Gentlemen, we now come to the events at Solon; events which, in their consequences, were far more serious than those we have been dealing with over the past two weeks. From the testimony we have heard we have been brought to the conclusion that the mutiny in Jullundur was started in the canteen through a conversation which consisted entirely of second hand reports culled from newspapers and letters of events supposedly taking place in Ireland and, in the case of private Hawes, stories from his personal experience whilst on leave. Rabble rousing remarks led Hawes to assert that what the English are supposedly doing in Ireland is what these men have been asked to do in India which, as far as I can see it, is merely to maintain law and order. The next question however was, "What are we going to do about it?" What are we going to do about it? Well... we have seen what they did about it. And we have seen the consequences of what they did about it. And it is highly unfortunate that this regrettable affair did not end there and then. We do not yet know exactly when the C Company men at Solon first heard of events in Jullundur. A letter written by Private Delaney and addressed to one of their number was intercepted and found to be a direct incitement to mutiny. No other possible interpretation can be put on it. We also know that privates Keenan and Kelly broke out of their barracks and made their way to Solon with the express purpose of carrying word of the mutiny. And, on arrival there, they were immediately placed under arrest and are being tried with the Solon men who stand before you today. Now, gentlemen, we know that the four men in the canteen at Jullundur were collectively responsible for the mutiny but, of the forty men arrested at Solon, one man above all others must stand out as guilty of the gravest charges. You will hear evidence leaving no shadow of doubt that this man actively sought for himself the role of ringleader. With calculated, cold-blooded, malicious engineering, he turned loyal troops into mutineers of the worst kind, fanning the natural grievances and resentments of the serving man into flames of armed insurrection and, whatever the men of Jullundur have said in defence of their actions, there is no possible defence for the men of C Company, Solon, except that some were led like sheep and some, unfortunately, like sheep to the slaughter. And for this - one man is guilty. And that one man is Private James Daly.

The LIGHTS have come up on DALY, who is now standing back against the door, and, as they fade on LLOYD, the bungalow is illuminated, the early morning sunlight streaming into the room.

EGAN	Is there nobody has a fag?
GLEESON	Any sign of the char-wallah?
DALY	No. But there's sign of something else. That bloody nappi's coming back.
FITZGERALD	Now what would he be wanting do you suppose?
GLEESON	He couldn't have got himself a new razor.
SEARS	If he has its too late.
GLEESON	Not for you, baby. I reckon you won't be needing a shave for another twelve months at least.

The NAPPI appears at the door. He carries an air of great excitement as he waits for one of the men to speak. They stand looking at him.

DALY	All right, let's be having it.

NAPPI	Big news, sir, very big news. *(He looks eagerly from one to the other as they wait)* The dhobi, sirs, he's hearing it so I'm running all the way at once, immediately, sirs, and telling you. The major, sirs, he's telling the Lieutenant, very big news from Jullundur.

GLEESON	They've been attacked?

NAPPI	No, sir, not attack. The Rangers, sir, they attack the British.

Silence.

FITZGERALD	*(Laughing)* The heat's gone to his head.

EGAN	You shouldn't have booted him so hard, Jimmy. You've knocked all the brains out of his arse.

NAPPI	No, sir, what I am telling you is truth please, sir. The Rangers make big trouble in Jullundur. They are saying no more fighting for England, not any more.

GLEESON	He can't be serious.

FITZGERALD	If he is serious then it's serious.

SEARS	Mutiny?

FITZGERALD	Aye, lad, that's about the size of it, mutiny.

DALY	The dhobi's lying.

NAPPI	Not lying, sir.

EGAN	What are we going to do?
GLEESON	What can we do? We don't know anything.
FITZGERALD	*(To DALY)* Your brother William's there in Jullundur.
EGAN	The one they call Sap? Sure now I never knew he was Jim's brother.
GLEESON	Did ye not? Could you not tell from the likeness?

This digression agitates SEARS who appeals to DALY.

SEARS	What are we going to do?
GLEESON	We don't know anything.

DALY grabs hold of the NAPPI.

DALY	Now think hard, you miserable bastard, exactly what was it the dhobi said the major said?
NAPPI	That is all, sir, big trouble in Jullundur.
GLEESON	You see? We don't know anything.

The NAPPI wriggles out of DALY's grip and streaks away.

SEARS	What are we going to do?
GLEESON	Nothing.
EGAN	Now is it not like working all night to get to the point and then having her tell you her husband's coming home any moment?
SEARS	Jimmy?
DALY	What?

They all turn to DALY. Silence.

DALY (*Shrugs*) It's not any affair of ours what happens in Jullundur.

GLEESON We don't know anything.

EGAN They are our mates there.

FITZGERALD Your brother William is there.

EGAN The one they call Sap.

DALY I'll tell you what, it's more than likely half a dozen lads have got it into their heads to get into trouble that's all.

FITZGERALD Is that all?

DALY Well how should I know?

GLEESON That's right. He doesn't know a thing more than the rest of us together and what we know is nothing.

EGAN Major Alexander knows something.

DALY Then go and ask Major Alexander.

FITZGERALD Or that snotty Lieutenant.

EGAN Which one? They're all snotty.

SEARS Someone's coming. It's John Oliver.

GLEESON Here?

OLIVER appears.

OLIVER Have youse heard?

DALY	*(Quietly)* Heard what?
OLIVER	They've arrested two Jullundur men.
EGAN	Two is it?
GLEESON	Well that's all right then.
FITZGERALD	Only two.
DALY	Didn't I tell youse?
OLIVER	They're in the guardroom right now. Jullundur men.
FITZGERALD	We know they're Jullundur men. But only two of them?
OLIVER	And is it a whole company ye'd be expecting?
GLEESON	From what the nappi said, a whole barracks.
OLIVER	And what would a whole barracks from over there be doing over here?
DALY	Here?
OLIVER	That's right. Haven't I just this minute been tellin' youse?
DALY	You didn't say here.
OLIVER	In the guardroom I said.
GLEESON	Our guardroom?
OLIVER	Who's else?
EGAN	We thought you meant they were in Jullundur.

DALY   Do you know what they're doing here?

GLEESON   Are you sure now there's only the two of them?

OLIVER   What's the matter with him?

DALY   What are they doing here?

OLIVER   They tried to break in and the guard spotted them. So they was put under arrest. But they started shouting about how there's big trouble in Jullundur.

GLEESON   Oh, Jesus!

DALY   What kind of trouble?

OLIVER   I didn't get it all do you know? But something about the freedom of Ireland and men put under arrest.

FITZGERALD   It's true then.

GLEESON   We don't know anything.

EGAN   We do, by God! We're just hearing it this very minute.

SEARS   What are we going to do?

There is the sound of a bugle. The men stand looking at DALY with OLIVER behind him. FITZGERALD finally breaks the silence.

FITZGERALD   We should get fell in.

DALY   *(To OLIVER)* We're not parading today. Tell the others, spread the world.

OLIVER   What?

FITZGERALD   Jim!

DALY   Those are our own in Jullundur. We have to stick by them. Are youse with me?

The men all look from one to the other, not knowing what to say.

GLEESON   Jim, maybe we ought to parade. Maybe we ought to wait.

DALY   No. If we're going to do it we're going to do it now.

The LIGHTS fade on the bungalow and come up on the court martial where MAJOR ALEXANDER is standing by the witness table facing LLOYD.

LLOYD   Major Alexander, as officer commanding C. Company, Solon, will you please tell us, as much and as accurately as you can remember, the events of July the first after the arrest of Keenan and Kelly.

ALEXANDER   Well... I had of course been informed of events at Jullundur so naturally I was on the lookout for any trouble. But unfortunately these two men managed to break into barracks before being spotted and shouted out a garbled sort of message while being marched away. It might not have been so bad however had the word not been passed on to Private Daly.

LLOYD   Why Daly?

ALEXANDER   Why?

LLOYD   Why 'not so bad'?

ALEXANDER   Oh, I see. Because this man took it upon himself to put two and two together and spread the

	message through the barracks. In consequence of this the men at first refused to parade, saying their action was a protest against the British in Ireland and that they were acting in support of the men - comrades was the word I think they used - in Jullundur.
LLOYD	But they did eventually parade.
ALEXANDER	If you want to call it that. The turnout of an undisciplined mob is what I'd call it.

The men from the barrack room march downstage and parade in what appears to be a perfectly normal manner.

DALY	Squad... Squad, halt!
ALEXANDER	Hmn. It gave me the opportunity at least of trying to drum some sense into them. *(Turning to the line)* You men, I tell you straight and make no bones about it, what you are doing today is more than foolishness. Your actions - mutinous actions - can lead only to dire consequences to yourselves. What do you hope to gain from this? Stop now while there is still time, still hope. For your own sakes, for the sake of your families back home. Can't you see how futile it all is? You will fail. You must fail, and no one will ever hear again either of you or your protest. Do you think for one moment your actions here can have the slightest effect on the British government? I tell you they will have no effect whatsoever.

DALY steps forward.

DALY	Sir, permission to speak, sir.

ALEXANDER grunts.

DALY	With respect, sir, I feel obliged to inform you

	that similar action will be taken by every Irish regiment in the British army and the news published in all the papers.
ALEXANDER	*(Turning to LLOYD)* I have no notion where he got this idea from but, whatever influence I might have had on the less determined of the mutineers, it was promptly wiped out by this man.
LLOYD	What happened then?
DALY	I have to inform you, sir that we have to place you and your fellow officers under arrest.
ALEXANDER	What!
DALY	You will be confined to your quarters under guard. I am sorry to have to do this, sir, but you will be treated with all respect due your rank and as a gentleman.

DALY steps back into line. The men turn and march away.

LLOYD	Were you ill-treated?
ALEXANDER	*(Pauses before he speaks)* If you mean, were we treated with violence then, no. But we most certainly were not treated like officers.
LLOYD	How do you mean?
ALEXANDER	*(Shouting angrily)* We were not treated with the respect due to officers!
LLOYD	The men have stated that they treated you with every courtesy and respect.
ALEXANDER	If you prefer to take the word of mutineers in preference to that of an officer of the British army.

LLOYD	Yes. What happened then, Major?
ALEXANDER	We were left under guard and the men returned to Daly's bungalow from which I later noticed they flew a tricolour.
LLOYD	The men remained inside? What do you suppose they were doing?
ALEXANDER	I can only presume they were deciding on their course of action, holding a council of war as it were.

The LIGHTS come up in the bungalow and we now see the men are armed. They sit around for a moment, not moving, no one wanting to say anything and then GLEESON, seated on a bed, hugging his rifle, looks up. LLOYD and ALEXANDER have left the stage.

GLEESON	What do we do now?
DALY	Sweat it out.
FITZGERALD	I'm doing that all right. Phew! That doesn't take much trying.
OLIVER	Do youse think we done the right thing?
DALY	What else could we do?
EGAN	We needn't have joined the bloody army for a start.
OLIVER	Major Alexander won't be forgiving us in a hurry.
EGAN	He hasn't forgiven his mother for bearing him.
DALY	There'll be no forgiving of any of us by anyone.

FITZGERALD   And that's a fact.

SEARS   Not unless we was to say we're sorry.

DALY   Are you?

SEARS   I don't know.

DALY   Are youse afraid?

SEARS   I don't know.

DALY   I am, lad.

They all turn to look at him.

DALY   And isn't it some kind of fool I'd be if I was not? But what's done is done. Do ye not think?

EGAN   It's a hell of a thing for a man to get himself into.

GLEESON   The thing is, to my way of thinking, how the hell are we going to get out?

FITZGERALD   We're not. Sink or swim we're all in it together and that's the God's honest truth.

SEARS   What can they do to us?

DALY   Have we lost?

OLIVER   What will we win?

EGAN   Not all the lads is behind us.

DALY   Those who aren't won't do anything.

FITZGERALD   The truth of it is we're on our own.

DALY   Are you not a great one for the truth now, Mick Fitzgerald?

FITZGERALD   Is it not?

DALY   No it is not.

EGAN   Tis us against the British Empire. What do you call those odds? If us hadn't helped the British knock down the Kaiser maybe he would have refereed.

DALY   What about the Jullundur men?

GLEESON   We don't know what's happening to the Jullundur men.

DALY   And what about our people at home?

OLIVER   Our people at home don't know what's happening to us.

DALY   But, if they did, would they not be behind us? Is it not for them that we're doing it?

OLIVER   What will we win?

DALY   What can we lose?

They don't like to think about this and there is a silence before FITZGERALD speaks.

FITZGERALD   Our lives.

DALY   If it's your skin you're so scared of, Mick, why did ye ever take it into your head to join the army at all? The day you joined the British army you said to them, here is my life, I give it to you without question to do with as you please. If it's in France you want me to die then I will die in France. If you should want me to die in Palestine that's where I'll die. If you want me to die in India, in India I will die. Is it not better you should die for Ireland's cause than for England's? Every soldier, man, every day of his life, might be called upon at any moment to die. He knows that. What then is so terrible about dying?

OLIVER	What will we win?

DALY	If we win only some sympathy for Ireland's cause, if we win only ears to listen, we will have won enough. At least our voices will have been heard. You can't light a fire without there's a spark first.

OLIVER	What if the spark goes out without lighting the fire?

FITZGERALD	How many of us are there? Thirty? Forty? Fifty at most? That's a terrible small spark in this big old world.

DALY	All right. All right. *(He looks from one to the other)* There's still time. If any of youse wants to back out, now's the time to say so. There's no one will stop ye. There's no one will point the finger at ye or call ye coward. Go now to the other side and no more will be said on it. *(Pause - then looking straight at him)* Sears?

They all turn to look at SEARS, the baby of them all. He, in turn, looks from one to the other. Finally he shakes his head and very softly.

SEARS	I'm for Ireland.

DALY looks around. No one moves. Finally.

FITZGERALD	The way I see it is, we're all for Ireland, and that's the truth of it.

DALY	By God, that's the truth of it!

He waits eagerly for some sort of reaction but the men remain still.

	Is it agreed then? We stay right here and sit it out. Sooner or later they're going to have to send troops against us. If they won't talk then we fight. Word will get around what has happened here and there'll be talk soon enough, in the army, in the papers, in the English parliament even. Anyway, I don't see as they're going to open up without talking first. No, there's little chance of that. Then, when we've had our say, we'll walk out meek as lambs, no harm done, and there's not so much they can do about that.
EGAN	Is there not? They can still shoot us for mutiny, even a meek and mild one. And, if they don't shoot us, we can get plenitude for life so we can. Yes.
GLEESON	Get what?
EGAN	Plenitude for life. Think about that.
GLEESON	I am thinking about it. My God, plenitude for life! Plenitude! Oh, Jesus! Penultude you mean, you silly ignorant bastard.
EGAN	Pe-nul-tude then.
DALY	Well, whatever...
GLEESON	Plenitude... oh, Jesus!
DALY	...Whatever does happen...
GLEESON	Plenitude...
DALY	Whatever happens, and I don't say I know what it's to be, we're going to be charged and court-

martialled, there's no doubt of that. So ye best be prepared.

GLEESON suddenly stops giggling to himself and shaking his head over Egan's ignorance.

GLEESON	I still don't know how it all happened. How did it happen? Do youse any of you know? And what about me ould woman? Oh, Jesus! What's me ould woman going to do if I'm rotting away in an English jail?
SEARS	And what about the mother?
DALY	The mother will be proud of you, son.
EGAN	And what about all them hordes of lovely women? Them that are always chasing me? All those lovely women, they're going to miss me something terrible.
FITZGERALD	They've been getting along well enough without you all the while you've been away.
EGAN	Begad, they'll be throwin' their lovely selves into the waters of the Liffy faster than you can count.
GLEESON	Oh, Jesus!
EGAN	And it's of absolute no use you sitting there calling on the Lord every two minutes. You can light thirty candles all at once but He'll not be getting you out of this mess, not while the English is here to stop Him so make up your mind to it.
DALY	I don't know so much. Talk of the Lord has brought his shepherd running to the flock.

PRIVATE HYNES appears in the doorway. He is armed with

rifle and fixed bayonet.

HYNES   Tis Father Baker. Do I let him in?

DALY   Of course you let him in.

HYNES turns away from the door and FATHER BAKER appears. The men all get to their feet.

BAKER   Do I talk to all of you? Or do I talk to you, Jim Daly? You seem to have been opening your mouth quite a lot of late.

FITZGERALD   Talk to Jim, Father. He'll speak for all of us.

BAKER   Will he now?

He moves into the room and makes himself comfortable on a bed.

                      A fine pickle you've got yourselves into. Well, having got into it, let's see if we can get you out again without too many ruffled feathers. What do you plan to do?

DALY   We wait.

BAKER   Wait? For what? The Day of Judgement?

DALY   For the English to come to us.

BAKER   Oh, they'll come all right.

HYNES   And we'll be ready for them

BAKER   With those? *(He nods towards a rifle)* They will save you will they?

FITZGERALD   Tis not ourselves we're after saving, Father.

BAKER   *(Angrily)* Talk! *(Quiet)* Maybe not. But I'm after saving ye. From yourselves first and then from the English. Then, when we've sorted that out, we'll have to stop for a while to consider the devil. It's a lot of work you're giving me.

The men laugh to break the tension.

Are you all little children that you know not what you do? Or what must surely happen to you? Look, I know you all; I'm one of your own. I know how you feel and why you feel it but what you are doing is wrong, believe me, in every way, most of all for yourselves.

HYNES What would you have us do? *(BAKER turns to him)* Father.

BAKER Well, firstly, take away the guard and release the officers.

DALY Why?

BAKER Because you've hurt their pride, that's why, and nothing hurts worse than bruised pride. If, of your own free will, you take off the guard at least you'll salvage something of their dignity. Secondly, hand over your weapons.

There is a chorus of "No's".

Yes! You are few in number, even less than the men in Jullundur. What can those do for you? Your resistance is in yourselves. You have no need of arms to bolster your cause. You can be wiped out to a man and take a lot of other good men with you. If you must rebel then do it without the threat of bloodshed because, once blood is spilled there is no going back, ever.

FITZGERALD He who puts his hand to the plough.

BAKER	Does so to till the soil, to make lovely things grow.

FITZGERALD	Are we not doing that?

BAKER	Not by the unnecessary taking of life, not by spilling blood, your own or anybody else's. Jim, you're a lad of sense, can you not see reason in my argument?

DALY nods.

Then do as I ask. If you all want to sit here and wait for events to take their course, do so, but not with rifles. Hand them over, Jim. Don't resist with violence. Give me your word on that.

A hullabaloo breaks out, everyone talking and arguing at once.

HYNES	You can't do it, Daly. It's playing right into their hands.

FITZGERALD	I think maybe Father Baker's right. We can't fight the whole bloody army and that's a fact.

EGAN	But if we give in now, what we've done will be nothing.

GLEESON	How do we know it will be anything anyway?

HYNES	I tell you its surrender.

SEARS	That's right.

GLEESON	Maybe we should be thinking about it at least.

BAKER rises to face DALY.

DALY	All right, Father, we'll do as ye ask on condition...

BAKER　　　　No conditions, Jim.

DALY　　　　All right. We'll do as you ask.

BAKER　　　　I have your word on it?

DALY　　　　You have my word, Father

They shake hands and BAKER leaves. LLOYD and ALEXANDER return. During their exchange the men file out of the bungalow with their rifles and return without them to resume their places.

ALEXANDER　　　　Shortly after the chaplain left the guard was removed and we were informed we need no longer consider ourselves under arrest. It seems he also managed to persuade them to hand over their arms and, if they must rebel, to do so by, how shall I put it...?

LLOYD　　　　Passive resistance?

ALEXANDER　　　　Hmn... Don't much like the phrase but I suppose that would describe it. Anyway, the arms were collected and locked in the magazine over which I set a heavy guard.

LLOYD　　　　You felt that was necessary.

ALEXANDER　　　　Of course.

LLOYD　　　　What did you do then?

ALEXANDER　　　　I telephoned headquarters for instructions.

LLOYD　　　　And what were your instructions?

ALEXANDER　　　　To wait for reinforcements.

LLOYD　　　　So you waited.

ALEXANDER　　　　We all waited.

LLOYD and ALEXANDER leave and the LIGHTS come up full on the barrack room. HYNES has taken the place of OLIVER. SEARS and DALY are drinking tea, the others, beer.

EGAN	If this isn't the longest day in the history of the world my name is not John Eugene Egan.
FITZGERALD	I wish it were St. Patrick's Day.
GLEESON	And why would you be wishing that?
FITZGERALD	Because then I could wear a shamrock.
GLEESON	And where in the length and breadth of this heathen country would you be finding a shamrock?
EGAN	And, even if you did, it would only be one weed growing on another. Is there nobody's got a fag?
HYNES	Well, the day's nearly over anyway.
FITZGERALD	It's going to be one hell of a long night and that's the truth of it.
EGAN	And are you going to get through it on a cup of tea, Jim Daly? You know it's a marvel to me that you've never taken to the beer. Do you not like it at all?

DALY shakes his head.

Have you never taken a drop in all your life?

DALY shakes his head again.

HYNES	You don't know what it is you're missing.
GLEESON	Sears! Sit down, for Christ's sake!

DALY   What do you say to a game of mukki bito. It'll help pass the time. Somebody light a lamp before it gets too dark in here.

GLEESON gets and lights a hurricane lamp. DALY drains the last of his tea and then hurls the dregs on to the floor. The men gather around.

SEARS   I'll play.

DALY   Right, choose your leaves.

HYNES   How much?

DALY   One anna each.

EGAN   Somebody lend me an anna.

SEARS   Here you are.

EGAN   Why thank you, lad. You'll get it back in no time at all, with interest. *(He places the anna on the floor)* That's my leaf.

SEARS   I'll take that one.

FITZGERALD   Will you believe it now but there's never a fly in sight.

EGAN   There must be. Hundreds of the bastards. I've got a feeling this is going to be my lucky night.

SEARS   *(Pointing upwards)* There's one!

DALY   Right, place your bets.

The rest of them put their coins on the floor.

(To SEARS) Right, bring him down, lad.

SEARS waves his arms and obviously brings down the fly

because, for the next half minute in absolute silence every head in unison follows the fly's course as it zooms about the room before finally landing on the floor.

EGAN   *(Whispering)* Do ye see that? Next to my leaf. He's landed right next to my leaf.

DALY   Next to it he might be but he's not on it.

FITZGERALD   And if he's got any sense he never will be.

EGAN   What do you suppose his name is?

GLEESON   What are you on about, you daft sod? Whoever heard of a fly having a name?

EGAN   If he hasn't got a name how can I tell him to sit on my leaf?

SEARS   You're not supposed to encourage him. That's not fair.

EGAN   If you put money on a racehorse you yell at it don't you? I know what, I'll call him Alexander.

The men like the idea of this and there is an excited yelling chorus of "Come on, Alexander!" "No, no, on mine!" "Would you believe it now? The silly bastard's walking away." "Come on, Alexander! Come on!" The excitement and noise is such that, at first, the men don't notice that OLIVER has entered the room. As they do the noise dies down with the fly still not having settled on a particular leaf. DALY turns to look around and up.

DALY   Where have you been?

OLIVER   Finding out things.

DALY   What things?

OLIVER   There's troops on their way to arrest us in the

	morning.
DALY	Well, that's no more than to be expected. *(He turns back to the game).*
OLIVER	There's more. You know the Lawrence Military School.
DALY	In Sanawar?
OLIVER	That's right. Well the boys have been put under arms.
HYNES	What!
OLIVER	Not all of them mind, only the older ones, from fourteen up.
DALY	You mean because of us?
GLEESON	I don't believe it!
OLIVER	Believe it or not, it's the truth so help me.
EGAN	The bastards! Putting lads under arms, mere babies. What for? To keep us in?
GLEESON	Where do they think we'll go? We're wearing British uniforms. That doesn't exactly make us popular in these parts. And there's none of us speaks the lingo. Anyway, do they suppose we're going to take a stroll over the Himalayas and walk home?
EGAN	Putting young lads under arms. Babies only. Like Sears.
SEARS	I am not a baby.
FITZGERALD	Bloody fools.

DALY	Maybe not so. I for one wouldn't fight a slip of a lad. Maybe they figured that out. So, if the lads want to keep us in, in we will be kept.
OLIVER	There's more. The band have been issued with rifles.
EGAN	Our band?
HYNES	Is that right?
OLIVER	Drummers, buglers, every man jack of them.
EGAN	But they're Connaughts! They're our own!
HYNES	It's our own they're turning against us.
GLEESON	That's a terrible thing to do.
HYNES	All right then, if that's the way they're going to play the game, how are we going to play it?
DALY	As we are.
HYNES	You're going to let them get away with it?
DALY	With what?
HYNES	I say we take back our rifles.
DALY	What for?
HYNES	To show them we're not going to give in as easy as they suppose.
DALY	No.
EGAN	Yes. We take back our rifles.
DALY	We can't do that.

HYNES   And why not?

EGAN   Give us a reason.

DALY   I gave my word to Father Baker. You all heard me give it. I'll not break it.

HYNES   Is that all?

DALY   I gave my word.

HYNES   I don't think that's all.

DALY   What more should there be?

HYNES   We're walking out unarmed against the guard. Are you afraid?

There is a long silence as DALY faces HYNES.

DALY   Fall in outside and follow me and I'll show you if I am a coward.

DALY leaves the room. The men follow. EGAN brings up the rear, turns at the door, returns to the room and picks up the annas which he pockets before hurrying out after the others.

An open space before the magazine which is in darkness. The men appear, led by DALY and, from the darkness, there is the sound of a hand slapped against the butt of a rifle and a voice.

SENTRY   Halt! Who goes there?

DALY   *(Stepping forward)* I am James Joseph Daly of Tyrell's Pass, Mullingar, County Westmeath, Ireland, and I demand ye to lay down your arms and surrender in the name of the Irish Republic.

The figure of the SENTRY is almost discernible in the darkness. He half turns and calls out.

SENTRY   Lieutenant Walsh!

From the darkness behind there is a flash and the crash of a service revolver. The men drop to the ground. One of them moves. It is SEARS. He gets to his feet and, clutching his chest which is bloodied, staggers forward.

SEARS   Bastards! Bastards!

DALY starts to his feet and makes to pull the lad back but is himself stopped by HYNES. The revolver cracks again. SEARS pitches backwards and rolls over. The rest of the mutineers get to their feet and stand facing the darkness which is the magazine.

SEARS lifts himself on his arms and screams out one word.

SEARS   Mother!

Then he falls forward on his face and lies still.

ACT TWO

Daly's CELL. DALY and FATHER BAKER in the position in which we left them. DALY is staring straight out in front and, after a moment of silence, BAKER lifts his head from his hand turns to look at him.

BAKER   What is it, Jimmy?

DALY   Hmn? It's me scar. It's hurting me. *(He gets to his feet and gently rubs his knee).*

BAKER   Is it a boyhood scar?

DALY   *(Shaking his head)* A souvenir you might call it, of France. *(He sits on the bench beside BAKER)* Father, I've written some letters. Would you be so kind and see they get there?

BAKER   Of course.

DALY takes a couple of letters from his tunic pocket and hands them over.

DALY   I was sixteen do you know when I joined the army. The mother, she wrote to the government and tried to get me out. My father was very angry. We quarrelled mightily. This one is the most important.

He is holding a third envelope and, although he could reread what he has written, it would be preferable to have the two men sit absolutely still while we hear Daly's MOTHER read the letter. This is the only opportunity in the play to hear a woman's voice. The letter is copied verbatim from the actual document.

MOTHER   October, Saturday. 1920. My address is in Heaven along with John - and God. My dearest Mother, I take this opportunity of writing to you to let you know the dreadful news that I am to be shot on Tuesday morning the 1st of November but what harm it is all for Ireland. I am not afraid to die but it is thinking of you I am that is all if you will be happy on earth I will be happy in Heaven I am ready to meet my doom the Priest is along with me when needed so you need not worry over me as I am going to my dearest home in Heaven but I wish to the Lord I had not started getting into this trouble at all I would be better off but it is done now and I have to suffer out of 62 of us I am the only one to put out of this world but I am ready to meet if God bless ye all hoping to see ye all in Heaven some day. I hope mother that you won't be put about but keep a good hart I know it is hard for you but what can be done now I am writing to Kitty and Dolly to let them know the Priest will send these letters to you all right I have not much to tell you as it is no good this is my last letter you will get from me and may God bless you Mother dear and the Bird *(His sister Bridie)* and Frank. Tell father I forgive him...*(The letter here has been destroyed by time)* I hope Paddy is well. Kisses to all. *(There are nine crosses)* I hope mother you will get a mass ready for me pray for a happy rest of your fond son Jim taking from you for the sake of his country Ireland. God bless Ireland and also you all at home. From your fond son Jim to dearest mother.

DALY hands over the envelope.

DALY	Do you think maybe I should have written to the lad's mother?
BAKER	I have done it.
DALY	I would not know what to say.
BAKER	I have done it as best I can, Jimmy.

DALY nods and goes back to his original position.

The scar's not hurting?

DALY shakes his head. But he still stares straight ahead, thinking.

What is it?

DALY   I was thinking, Father, do you reckon it was, it was my... do you think at all I was to blame for the boy dying?

A SPOT snaps on LLOYD.

LLOYD   Gentlemen, you have heard the evidence. Only one man can possibly be held responsible for the death of private Sears and also, gentlemen, for the death of an innocent bystander, a soldier who had done nothing more harmful than visit the canteen for a cup of tea and, on returning to his bungalow, was caught up in the battle, shot in the head and instantly killed. And just think, gentlemen, had Father Baker not rushed in and implored all concerned to stop, how many more might have died that night? But, if private Daly is not responsible for these two deaths then, may I ask, who is? Lieutenant Walsh? Lieutenant McSweeney? The two men in command of the guard that night. Two young officers of exceptional merit without a black mark to their names.

The LIGHTS now come up on the court martial and we see ALEXANDER still at the witness table. DALY is downstage.

Daly, you have heard the testimony of Major Alexander, are there any questions you would like to put to him? Daly!

DALY	Sir?
LLOYD	You are entitled to question the testimony you have just heard. If you think anything has been said against you which should not have been said then it is up to you to cross-examine the witness.
DALY	Yes, sir.
LLOYD	Well?
DALY	Major Alexander, sir... after the fighting, is it not true that we took the hurt men to the camp hospital?

ALEXANDER frowns, glances towards LLOYD, then back to DALY. He is hesitant.

ALEXANDER	Yes.
DALY	And is it not true, sir, that we stayed there while the doctor saw John Egan's wound taken care of?
ALEXANDER	I don't know what...
DALY	Is it not true, sir?
LLOYD	Daly, is there some point to this line of questioning?
DALY	And when Egan was resting easy and we knew for certain poor Sears and the other one was both dead, did I not ask for a drink or something being as I was that thirsty?
LLOYD	Daly, I really don't...
DALY	With respect, sir, you said I could ask questions, sir. And, when the doctor handed me a glass of

	something, was it not Father Baker who said to let him drink a bit of it first? And when Father Baker tried to take the glass did the doctor not spill it on the floor?
LLOYD	Daly, this is doing your case no good whatsoever.
DALY	Why did the doctor do that, sir?

ALEXANDER is looking very ruffled. He looks again at LLOYD, at the long table, back to DALY.

	And then didn't Father Baker say, "Doctor, what were you trying to do?"
LLOYD	*(Angrily)* Daly, let me clarify this point. Are you seriously trying to tell this court that a deliberate attempt was made on your life?
DALY	I am, sir. Because didn't Father Baker himself believe it? Did he not stay in our bungalow that night and sleep in Mick Fitzgerald's bed which is next to mine in case something else happened.
LLOYD	*(Quickly)* Major Alexander, you are not obliged to answer any question you think may incriminate you.

This is quite the wrong thing to say. ALEXANDER is almost apoplectic.

ALEXANDER	Incrim...!
LLOYD	You need say nothing.
DALY	Somebody must have ordered the doctor to do it.
ALEXANDER	*(Finding his voice and thundering)* This is preposterous! No such order was ever given or so much as contemplated.

DALY   Suggested then. Suggested that if I was put out of the way the mutiny would stop that instant.

LLOYD   Do you realise, man, what you are saying? You are suggesting that an officer of the British army would attempt to poison you.

DALY   Yes, sir.

LLOYD   Major Alexander, was there ever, in any conversation you might have had with the doctor, any suggestion that an attempt should be made on the life of Private Daly?

ALEXANDER   Never!

LLOYD   This supposed incident at the hospital, were you present at the time?

ALEXANDER   I was not.

LLOYD   Then this evidence is hearsay and cannot be submitted. It must be struck from the record. Daly, your questions to a witness must be directly concerned with the evidence already given by that witness. You cannot make wild allegations or strike off at new tangents. Keep to the point.

DALY   I would have thought it a point all right that someone tried to have me murdered. If I am not permitted to talk about someone trying to kill me what is the point in me trying to talk about me killing someone else? Someone who I did not kill.

LLOYD   You are not accused of killing anyone.

DALY   No, but I am accused of being responsible am I not? And is that not the same thing altogether?

	If the doctor's plan to kill me off at the hospital had worked who would be standing here now accused of my death? Would it not be Major Alexander for sure? But Major Alexander would be standing here for the whole of the British army, the British government, the British Empire, as sure as I am standing here now for the whole of Ireland.
LLOYD	Daly, are you deliberately trying to alienate the sympathies of this court?
DALY	What sympathies, sir?
LLOYD	Any that the members of this court might have for you.
DALY	Why should they have, sir?
LLOYD	If for no other reason because they are men.
DALY	Begging your pardon, sir, they're soldiers first and tis not as a man I am being tried. It's as Ireland that you would murder me. It's as Ireland that I am surely going to die.
LLOYD	If wild accusations can do your cause no good, private Daly, then neither can rabid political speeches. Now, have you any further questions to put to this officer?

Pause.

DALY	No, sir.
LLOYD	Have you anything more to say?

Pause.

DALY	No, sir, I have nothing more to say.

The lights on LLOYD and ALEXANDER fade and the two men leave the stage. DALY remains where he is and HAWES enters downstage in front of a plain wall. He walks up to DALY.

HAWES Tis James Daly is it? *(He holds out his hand)* Hawes, Joseph Hawes of Kilrush in County Clare. Welcome to Dagshai prison.

They shake hands.

We heard news you was coming in today. How many of youse are there?

DALY Forty.

HAWES And of us there's forty-eight.

DALY Eighty-eight in all.

HAWES There must be something in that now if I could put my mind to what it could be.

DALY Do you know my brother William? The one they call Sap?

HAWES Aye, I know him.

DALY He's here?

HAWES No, he was with us at the very first but he was never with us after that.

DALY *(Nods)* He was always the careful one was William. I'm glad.

HAWES That there's not the two of youse you mean.

DALY *(Nods again)* I was thinking of the mother. She's lost two. She's going to lose another. It would be more than pity is worth were she to lose four.

HAWES   Who is it says she's going to lose the third?

DALY   Do you doubt it?

Silence.

HAWES   Of course you'll be telling us what happened in Solon. We've heard bits and pieces from the guards, those that want to talk to us. I'm sorry about the lad.

DALY   What's it like here?

HAWES   Oh, you'll like it here right enough. Dagshai's a great old prison so it is. I won't do you a conducted tour right this minute but it might just interest you to know that this place has not been used at all since 1916. Did you already know that?

DALY   No. Why is that?

HAWES   Well now, the why of it is very interesting do you see; us being in it as it were. Seems it was a jail for natives until too many of them died off in the place so it was condemned. But it's good enough for the Irish wouldn't you say? And you'll like the food well enough. Black tea and bread in the morning and bully for supper. Ah, but that's an appetizing thought for a hungry man so it is.

DALY   How long do you suppose they'll keep us here?

HAWES   Well now, who's to say? Seeing its three months and they've only just got round to taking the summary of evidence.

DALY   Is that right? How do they do that?

HAWES	Well it's rather like taking a deposition in a court at home. They marched us to a building outside the jail and then, in front of us, every man who is gong to swear against us, and a lot of them are our own, evidence was taken from them. Then, just before the trial, we'll each get a typed copy of that evidence.
DALY	What for?
HAWES	So as we can read it, those of us what can read, and there's not so many can. Are Keenan and Kelly with youse?
DALY	They are. We've been in Sulkut, and some in Puna.
HAWES	Aye, so I heard. They had nowheres in Dagshai to put you do you see? Not till they got the east wing redecorated specially.

They start to pace the yard. Other PRISONERS appear. FITZGERALD, LALLY, SWEENY.

	One thing I'll say for Dagshai, and it's about the only thing I'll say for it, it's at least better than where they had us for the first week. Did ye hear tell of it?
DALY	No.
HAWES	There might be only forty-eight of us now. There was four hundred and fifty when we marched out of Jullundur.
DALY	What happened?
HAWES	If I tell you a story will you listen to it?
DALY	I want to hear.

HAWES	Well it was like this do ye see...

LLOYD returns to his place and COLONEL JACKSON to the witness table.

	It was about four o'clock in the afternoon as I recall.
LLOYD	That was the day arranged, the 1st of July.
JACKSON	Yes.
HAWES	And there we saw the British troops advancing on our barracks in battle order. They had come at last. You know Jullundur, Daly, its open space so there was plenty of room for them to manoeuvre.
FITZGERALD	How many of them was there?
JACKSON	Two battalions, The Seaforth Highlanders and the South Wales Borderers.
DALY	*(Laughing)* The Welsh and the Scots by God.
JACKSON	Also a company of machine gunners.
HAWES	And don't forget the artillery. May the saints preserve us but they did us proud. Tis not for nothing they call us the devil's own. When the first of them got to the main guard where the arms and ammunition is stored, our guard presented arms in the name of the Irish Republic.
JACKSON	They then grounded their arms and rejoined the ranks of the mutineers who had already fallen in under their own committee.

Some of the Jullundur prisoners group themselves behind HAWES.

HAWES	Which is what we agreed on.
JACKSON	*(Uncomfortable)* Yes.
HAWES	And then we marched out, four deep, all four hundred and fifty of us, to march to the special camp two miles outside the barracks, as we had agreed.

A number of men wearing the uniforms of the South Wales Borderers line up on either side of the group of prisoners. JACKSON and HAWES confront each other.

	You broke your word to us. What are the soldiers doing here?
JACKSON	I'm sorry, Hawes, I couldn't take any chances.
HAWES	Is that why there's Lewis guns at all the crossroads?
JACKSON	Yes. It was my duty as I saw it not to take any chances.
LALLY	You broke your word.
JACKSON	You are mutineers.
LALLY	We are proud men.
JACKSON	Yes. I did not want to do it but what guarantee had I that you would keep your side of the agreement?
HAWES	A treaty is a treaty. Honour is honour.
JACKSON	You have forfeited your honour.
HAWES	No, sir. You have forfeited yours.

JACKSON	I had no guarantee I tell you. How could I know that, once out of the barracks, you wouldn't cause as much trouble as you could?
SWEENY	What kind of trouble? And where would we go?
JACKSON	Damn it! I had to have some form of protection!
HAWES	Hardly cricket, colonel. Hardly cricket.
JACKSON	Cricket? You can't handle a mutiny like a game of cricket.
HAWES	More like a hurling match wouldn't you say?
LLOYD	So the march to the specially prepared camp passed without incident.
HAWES	And what was their specially prepared camp but a flat space about... hmn... two hundred yards square, with barbed wire all round and some tents. We marched in through a gap in the fence where there was an armed guard and there was machine gun posts covering each side. So there we was like fish in the net.
LLOYD	Did you have any further contact with the prisoners?
JACKSON	I did. There was an unfortunate incident involving Major Payne.
LLOYD	Incident?

The stage now becomes a compound though DALY remains on one side and LLOYD and JACKSON on the other.

JACKSON	The following morning the men were paraded in a compound outside the camp. Major Payne, accompanied by a number of South Wales Borderers, addressed them. Afterward I had

the mutineers marched back to camp and considered the incident closed.

HAWES   Colonel Jackson, sir, was it never told you why Major Payne called us out in the first place?

JACKSON Well, yes... to make a final appeal for you to give up and return to duty.

SWEENY   Is that what you call it?

MAJOR PAYNE and a LIEUTENANT enter and PAYNE addresses the men.

PAYNE   You men... you don't have to be told who I am... Major Payne. Like yourselves I am a Connaught. Though, unlike yourselves, I still believe in the regiment to which we all belong and which we should all serve but which you have shamed and dishonoured. I am going to call out twenty names. Those men whose names I call will line over there. *(Pointing)* Flannery... *(No one moves)* Sweeny... *(No one moves)*... Hawes... Moran... Lynch... Delaney, Gogarty, Lally, Scanlon, Willis. (*No one has moved*). All right, I'll start again and it will be the better for you if you remember who you are and who I am. When I give an order I expect it to be obeyed. Flannery, Sweeny, Hawes, Moran. *(No one moves)*. Do you stupid bastards not think I know you? And know you for what you are? What do you call yourselves? Irishmen? You are a disgrace to Ireland. Scum! That's what you are. And lower than scum. Soldiers? A flea-bitten mangy pariah could fight better than the lot of you put together. Not one of you is fit to clean out a native latrine being worse than shit yourselves. Maggots have more reason to be alive. Now step out here at the double!

Apart from a certain restlessness at the flow of invective, no man moves. PAYNE *turns to the* LIEUTENANT *and there is a whispered conversation. He looks back at the prisoners and points. The prisoners all look at the man he is pointing to. Then they watch the* LIEUTENANT *cross over to the Borderers. There is another whispered conversation, the* LIEUTENANT *turns and marches back to the prisoners followed by the Borderers. The prisoners close ranks about the man pointed out. As the* LIEUTENANT *and Borderers go in to try and get him out a fracas develops, a rough melee as the mutineers close around them.* PAYNE *flies into an even more towering rage.*

PAYNE   Out! Out! Come out of there!

The LIEUTENANT *and* BORDERERS *retire. Some of them hurt. Those who have lost their rifles have them thrown out after them and suffer the indignity of having to reclaim them.*

                     Fall in!

The BORDERERS *scramble into line.*

PAYNE   Five rounds, stand and load.

Pulls a handkerchief from his pocket and turns to the mutineers.

                     I'm going to shoot you, you stupid bastards. Who the bloody hell do you think you are? Any of you? *(Turning to his men)* When I drop this handkerchief fire and spare no man. Shoot them down like dogs.

SWEENY   You can do your bloody best.

There is the sound of a long hard blast on a whistle and JACKSON *moves in between the parties.*

JACKSON   *(Furious)* Major Payne, who gave you orders to do this? Get away out of it and take those men with you.

PAYNE   The prisoners were becoming threatening, Colonel.

JACKSON   They were? Against armed men? (*To the LIEUTENANT*) Get them out of here.

LIEUTENANT   Sir!

He turns to the Borderers and orders them off. JACKSON watches then turns back to PAYNE and looks down at the handkerchief.

JACKSON   Are you sweating, major?

It is an awkward moment for PAYNE. He stands staring at JACKSON then screws up the handkerchief in his clenched fist.

PAYNE   With your permission, colonel.

Turns on his heel and goes. The prisoners break up, HAWES moving downstage. JACKSON goes back to the witness table.

HAWES   And do you remember, sir, what it was you said to us?

JACKSON   No, I don't recall.

HAWES   Did you not say, "I am sorry for this and, in future, nothing like it will happen?"

JACKSON   Yes, I did say that.

HAWES   Why, sir?

JACKSON   Because Major Payne had acted without any authority and without reference to me. I knew nothing of his intentions.

HAWES   Was it not also, sir, because Major Payne was

	blind drunk?
DALY	If it hadn't been for the colonel riding up…
LALLY	Blowing his whistle like a whole tribe of bearded Sikhs was on his tail.
DALY	Would there have been shooting do you suppose?
HAWES	There would have been slaughter.
DALY	God help us, the man must have been mad.
FITZGERALD	We're all mad and that's the truth of it.
HAWES	There's more ways of killing a cat than drowning it and more ways of killing a mutineer than shooting him. Did they not break the most of us? All our fighting comrades, where are they now? There's only the eighty-eight left.
DALY	We are enough.
FITZGERALD	It's a small spark.
HAWES	What?
FITZGERALD	A small spark to light a big fire, only eighty-eight.
DALY	What happened?
HAWES	Well, in the camp, there must have been thirty, forty taken off with the heat in the first few days and more giving themselves up to the sentries. No one tried to stop them. Anyone was free to go. The heat was something terrible so it was. No shelter except the tents.
FITZGERALD	Stinking canvas, it burns with the sun.

HAWES	So doctor Carney, he tells the colonel he won't be held responsible for the state of us and we're all marched back to number five bungalow where they've put barbed wire all round.
DALY	All of you in one bungalow?
HAWES	Jim, you've heard tell of the black hole of Calcutta, well I reckon I know what it was like in that place. Two days we was in that bungalow on bread and water and crowded so close a man could hardly move and piss and shit all over the place and these two priests coming to see us, telling us how we must change our minds, for is it not a terrible thing for a catholic to break his oath to a protestant king.
FITZGERALD	Were they Irish priests?
HAWES	So they said but I've a mind they was from Liverpool or some such place. Anyway we gave them our answer to take back to General Munro and they didn't like that. Neither did the general because the next day the Highlanders come roaring into the bungalow and routed forty-seven of us outside.
DALY	Did you not resist?
HAWES	Do you resist bayonets and clubs? At least no more than you can help it. I felt for sure this time it was the shooting, but they put us in leg-irons and drove us in lorries to another compound. Jim, I tell you, this time they thought they would break us for sure. Not even a stinking hot tent to keep the sun off us. Just a space and four walls and a machine gunner sitting in the corner under his shade. Two days they left us there without food or water. By God it was a terrible mess. Some of the men were

	pitiful to see. The second day doctor Carney comes to the place and looks at each man. "Stick it out, Hawes," he says, "I'll get you out of here as quick as I can."
FITZGERALD	Is that right?
HAWES	Am I not tellin' youse the story and not a word of a lie in it? Half an hour after the doctor has gone, an officer marches into the compound and asks us again to surrender. We told him what to do with himself and then the lorries came and took us back to barracks. If I live to see old age I tell you I'll never forget that place. To see men hold their little tunics over their heads trying to keep off the sun and dropping like flies, and the skin all blistered and falling off them, and their lips all swollen so they couldn't open their mouths. By God, I'll never forget that. And the others, they saw us coming back. We was marched into the guardhouse right opposite number five and the men stood there and watched. You could see on their faces what they was thinking. Next morning about ten o'clock in comes the colonel and the officers and the men are ordered in the name of the king to fall in under their respective officers. We shouted to them from the cells not to obey but I think maybe they remembered the look of us from the night before and they scrambled like a lot of sheep to get fell in, all that is but one man, Willis. Think of that, Jim, only one man. So Major Payne leaves his position and goes up to Willis. We could hear every word he said because he said it loud enough for the whole barracks to hear. "Willis," he says, 'you and I fought in the trenches together, why are you being so foolish? These men in the cells are going to their deaths. I will give you five minutes to consider and if you fall in with the loyal men I will do everything I can for you.'

Do you know, there wasn't a sound for about a minute. Not one single man moved. Everyone was just stood there looking at Willis. Then he says, "I would rather die with the men over in the cells, no matter what kind of death it is, than fall in under you with this shower of bastards here." You should have heard the noise then. Oh, Jesus, you should have heard it! Every man in the cells cheering his head off. Yes, even the men with their lips all cracked and swole up, cheering for Willis, and the others just standing there as Willis is marched into the guardhouse. Do you know what they did then? Just to show the sheep they was sheep the sergeants drilled them in that heat for half an hour where we could watch them doin' it. But they was a little bit disappointed because we didn't even bother to watch. That same evening an escort of Connaught Rangers took us in lorries to the railway and we was on our way here in the prison train, the forty-eight of us that was left. And that's how it was.

FITZGERALD   By God, is that not a story now to make a man proud?

DALY   What happens now?

HAWES   They'll keep us waiting a bit longer I reckon. You lot will have to go through this summary of evidence business. Then we'll be court martialled.

FITZGERALD   Do you reckon on them shooting us?

HAWES   Oh, yes, some of us. Maybe twenty, maybe ten, but some of us.

DALY   They can do their best. We've got this far, there's no going back now. They can't break us.

HAWES	They'll try. They'll keep on trying.
DALY	*(Shakes his head)* They can't break us now.
HAWES	Time drags heavy, Jim. When you've nought to do but think, time drags heavy. And they want you to feel dirty. We've nothing but the shirts on our backs. There's no soap, no towels, nothing. They send a barber in once a week to shave and cut hair.
DALY	Well I only hope he's a better nappi than ours at Solon. Do you think maybe the English were paying him to try and cut my throat?
FITZGERALD	No fear of that, Jim, he loved you like a brother and that's the truth.
HAWES	No fear of this one cutting your throat either. He believes in Ghandi. He's always on to telling about it. I seen Ghandi once. He's not a powerful big spark either, not to look at anyway. Did youse never see him? Only so high he is... *(Indicating with his hand)* and no meat on him at all. Ugly little runt of a creature, even his bandy legs you wonder how he's got the strength to walk on them, and these people, they follow him like he's twelve Popes rolled into one. He tells them, lie down on the railway line and stop the trains and, by God, they do just that. They lie down and have to be carried off before the trains can move. Now this man Ghandi, he's going to give the king of England a terrible headache, that's for sure.
DALY	I would like to see him.
FITZGERALD	We never thought of that.

DALY and HAWES look at him

	Sitting on the railway line.
DALY	If we had they'd have just gone on running over us.
FITZGERALD	Sometimes do you know, Jim Daly, I've a mind you want the English to shoot you.
HAWES	That Ghandi, he'd kiss the wheels of the train as they was squashing him. I tell you he's a saint that man. Isn't it a pity now he's not a catholic? What a grand martyr he would make.
DALY	Josie, do you think what we've done is wrong? From the church's way of thinking I mean.
HAWES	By all that's holy it never is! If they shoot us it's straight to heaven we'll be going make no mistake about it.
DALY	Not if the English can help it.
FITZGERALD	That's right. They'll dispatch a rider to St. Peter with special orders not to let in the Irish and, if he disobeys, they'll send up the artillery. Not to mention the Scots and the Welsh.
DALY	Or, maybe, they'll sit on the heavenly railways lines not to let our trains go through.

Although this is said quite seriously, the men start to laugh. DALY, surprised, looks at them and joins in. DEACON appears and the laughter stops as the men turn to face him and wait.

HAWES	*(Quietly)* One thing you've got to say for them, they don't give up easy. Them and their bloody bulldogs.
DEACON	*(Clears his throat)* Men... I am here to make a last minute appeal to you all, a personal appeal. I

have not been instructed by higher authority do so but I come here as your commanding officer and, I hope, someone you can trust and look on as a friend. *(He pauses for a reaction but there is no response)* This is no place for a Ranger.

DALY | Then why did you put us here?

DEACON | You put yourselves here.

HAWES | It's no place for a man.

DEACON | True. I agree with you. And there is no need for you all to be here. You could be back in your barracks with your comrades.

HAWES | I doubt they'd take it kindly if we was to walk in now.

DEACON | You could be comfortable, able to move about, visit the cinema, the bazaar, canteens. Beer and cigarettes. *(Pause)* Well what about your families?

DALY | What about them?

DEACON | How are they going to feel when they hear what has happened to you?

DALY | What has happened to us?

DEACON | In God's name, man, can't you see? Can't you try and understand? Your position is hopeless. You were a lost cause even before you started. Your protest means nothing.

DALY | It means everything.

DEACON | Nothing I tell you. You'll be court-martialled, you will be sentenced, and nothing more will be heard of the whole affair I promise you. Not one

	of you will be remembered. You will be buried in obscurity and your names forgotten. Not a word of your protest will ever be heard.
DALY	With respect, colonel, you're wrong. It already has been heard because we've made it, and too many ears have listened even if they have, out of cowardice, betrayed us.
DEACON	Out of commonsense.
DALY	Perhaps their cowardice was meant to be, so that they could talk for us when we are buried in obscure graves and cannot talk for ourselves.
DEACON	You're playing at being heroes. What will that get you? Listen to me carefully. Tomorrow a brigadier general will be coming to talk to you.
HAWES	*(A sarcastic whistle)* The big brass!
DALY	Why so big for a silent protest I wonder.
DEACON	He will make an appeal to you. He will ask you to fall in and march with him out of this place - free men. Now take that chance I beg of you. It's the last you will ever get.
HAWES	When the brigadier general comes to us tomorrow and says what you are saying today and we decide to fall in and march out of here, free men as call it, will that be all of us?

Despite himself, DEACON cannot help glancing in DALY's direction. The look does not go unnoticed.

DEACON	Yes, yes, of course.
HAWES	I suppose it would be too much to be asking for a tiny miracle now. I mean that all the charges will be dropped.

DEACON	There will be some charges of course.
DALY	Then we will hardly be free men.
DEACON	The charges will be different, not so serious. Only show a court-martial you are sorry for what you have done, for what has happened.
DALY	Repent and ye'll be saved, is that it?
DEACON	The court will be only too pleased to show leniency.
DALY	Why?
DEACON	Why? Because you will be able to return to duty as good soldiers, the good soldiers you have always been until this. But if you refuse to knuckle... I mean refuse to listen to reason, God knows what'll happen to you.
DALY	Who will be charge of the court-martial, sir?
DEACON	What difference does that make?
HAWES	I hear rumours it will be General Sir Sydney Lawford.
DEACON	Who told you that?
HAWES	Oh, I know a marvellous great deal about the British army. Have I not served it long and well?
DEACON	Then go on serving it.
DALY	No, sir. We cannot do that. It is time to serve our own.
DEACON	That may be but I am telling you for the last time, this is not the way to do it.

DALY   Tell us a better.

Silence.

HAWES   And the judge advocate will be Major Tucker.

DEACON   Who is coming with me? *(Silence)* Will you take your chance tomorrow? *(Silence)* Very well, on your own heads be it. I am sorry for you.

He turns and stalks away. For a moment there is stillness then DALY lets out an audible sigh.

DALY   I am twenty-six years old.

The LIGHTS fade and come up on LLOYD.

LLOYD   Gentlemen, these past two weeks have been long and difficult. None of us can feel pleased that we were called upon to undertake this task. However, we have tried to discharge our duty with fairness and to the very best of our ability. Gentlemen, we have been facing an episode almost meaningless, baffling in its lack of logic, but an episode that could bring the name of a proud fighting regiment into disrepute. We have heard evidence from a number of officers, from the military police and from N.C.O.'s and private soldiers, one time comrades of the men accused. When they have bothered to take any interest in the proceedings of this court, we have also heard the cross-examination of witnesses by the defendants. And precisely what, gentlemen, does this cross-examination add up to? Nothing but counter-accusation, accusation mainly of maltreatment after arrest and while awaiting trial. I will not dwell on this. It is not the witnesses who have been on trial. The men who are on trial however, the men charged, have no defence whatsoever.

They have admitted to the separate parts they played in the mutiny and all they can summon up in justification of their actions is the pleading of a cause, a zealous nationalism, a half-baked, misinformed intrusion into politics. For the thirty-two Jullundur men tried in the first week you have been magnanimous enough to recommend, that those men who you have perceptively identified as being influenced by the ringleaders, be returned to their units. I am sure the sentences you will pass on the remainder will show equally the generosity of this court. But in this, the second week, we have been dealing with the hard core of the mutiny, the men who started this abortive attempt at political blackmail and who have maintained their stubborn unrepentence and continued defiance in the face of all offers made to them. Of course it is not for me to overstep the mark and direct you as to your verdict. That is the province of the judge advocate. But I could not, as prosecuting council, feel more confident that the guilt of these sixteen men has been conclusively proved. They are guilty beyond redemption and, ideals or not, one cannot even contemplate a plea for mercy. Thank you, gentlemen.

LLOYD turns to face his table and go through his paper as HAWES enters downstage. At the same time LIEUTENANT SMYTH, carrying an attaché case and accompanied by a SERGEANT, enters, marches up to HAWES and hands him a letter. HAWES looks at the buff envelope, turning it over in his hands.

SMYTH   I'm sorry, Hawes, to be handing you this.

HAWES   On His Majesty's Service. Well... *(He rips open the envelope and takes out the document, reads it and then looks up).* It's an invitation to a shooting party. Isn't that nice?

SMYTH	I would hardly consider it a matter for jokes, Private Hawes.
HAWES	No, you're right. It wouldn't be considered the best of taste now would it?

SMYTH turns to go.

HAWES	Smyth.

He turns back.

	How many of these little letters do you have in your postbag there?
SMYTH	*(A pause)* Well, from now on, those of you under sentence of death will be kept separate from the other so you will know anyway. There's five of you altogether.

HAWES waits to be told.

	Gogarty, Moran, Delaney and Flannery.
HAWES	Flannery! So his turning king's evidence didn't do him any good. Well I'm not surprised at that. And what about the rest?
SMYTH	Oh, they won't know for some time yet what it's to be.
HAWES	But at least they know it won't be the shooting.
SMYTH	There might not have been any shooting if you'd been sensible, if you'd recognised the court, had someone to speak for you.
HAWES	There was no one to speak for us but ourselves. *(Pause)* Five of us.

SERGEANT   There'll be more soon.

HAWES   The Solon men you mean.

SERGEANT   Mark my words, it'll be a full postbag next week.

SMYTH   Sergeant!

SERGEANT   Sir? *(Realising)* Yes, sir.

The SERGEANT marches away followed by SMYTH. HAWES stands looking down at his envelope.

HAWES   On His Majesty's Service.

LIGHTS. LLOYD turns away from his table.

LLOYD   Gentlemen, in this the third week, we have heard evidence about the most outrageous and, I might add, the saddest episode in this whole affair. In a sorry catalogue of events that has brought so much discredit to the name of the Connaught Rangers nothing - nothing - approaches the enormity of the attack on the magazine at Solon. "I am James Joseph Daly of Tyrell's Pass, Mullingar, County Westmeath, Ireland, and I demand that you lay down your arms and surrender in the name of the Irish Republic". A rash, utterly stupid, insane adventure that led to the death of an innocent bystander and a young life thrown needlessly away. I do not presume, for one moment, to understand the madness behind this action but there can be no possible doubt that Private James Daly and all those men at Solon who followed him are, without exception, guilty of the gravest charges and therefore, gentlemen, deserving of the gravest penalty.

HAWES   All those men... Smith, Oliver, Egan, Hynes, Fitzgerald, Keenan, Kelly, Daly... and that makes thirteen of us altogether. There must be something in that somewhere but I don't like to think about it.

LIGHTS change and we are now on the verandah of the officers' mess. DEACON enters. He is in mess kit and carries a brandy glass. He stands for a moment, thinking. JACKSON enters, also in mess kit, carrying a brandy and smoking a cigar.

JACKSON Too stuffy in there for you?

DEACON *(Shaking his head)* I wanted to think.

JACKSON Oh, I'm sorry. Shall I leave you?

DEACON No no, I'll go back in a moment. I was never a great one for dinner parties though, not even my own.

JACKSON Pity. Congratulations anyway. An excellent burra khana. An excellent cigar. An excellent brandy.

DEACON *(Smiling)* Better than general Munro's?

JACKSON Now now, you wouldn't want me to be disloyal.

DEACON's smile disappears.

Oh, I really am very sorry. That was a bit of a faux pas.

DEACON shakes his head, indicating that it doesn't matter.

You're worried.

DEACON No. Apart from a few questions in the house, it's all over. I presume that's what you're referring to.

JACKSON I thought Lloyd handled himself jolly well.

DEACON   Yes, indeed he did. A good man that, one of the best. Must remember to mention it to him.

JACKSON   I think we can agree the trial couldn't have been more fair.

DEACON   The pity of it is that there had to be a trial in the first place. No, the question I keep asking myself is, why did it have to happen to us? Why the Rangers?

JACKSON   The luck of the draw, old man. You know what they say, one rotten apple.

DEACON   Well I have to admit it's beyond me. Even putting myself in their place, trying to see it from their point of view, it's still beyond me.

JACKSON   You can't.

DEACON   What?

JACKSON   Put yourself in their place. You can't think their way, no more than you can think like a Pathan or a Punjabi. Maybe that's why we'll always have scraps. A man can no more get under another man's skin than he can jump out of his own.

DEACON   Yes, perhaps you're right. Some fine men there though, Jackson, some damn fine men... *(He lifts his glass and drinks)*.

JACKSON   They were given every chance to come round. We went as far as we possibly could while there was still time.

DEACON   Yes.

JACKSON   Supposing the mutiny had got out of hand.

	Supposing it had spread to other regiments. I don't like to think about it.
DEACON	Yes, you're quite right. As it is some of us have come out of this a little scarred.

PAYNE enters.

| PAYNE | Good evening, sir. |

DEACON takes JACKSON's glass.

DEACON	Your glass is empty, Jackson. Excuse me. *(He exits).*
PAYNE	Colonel Jackson... I wanted to speak to you, sir, about...
JACKSON	Not now.
PAYNE	I would like...
JACKSON	Not now, Major!
PAYNE	I hear the death sentences have been commuted to penal servitude.
JACKSON	I'm glad of it.
PAYNE	No, it's all wrong. You don't snuff out trouble of this sort by being kind. Shoot the bastards.
JACKSON	Major Payne, you forget yourself. And I don't think being soft has anything to do with it. From a purely practical point of view the fewer martyrs the better. Penal servitude for life is hardly a soft sentence and, at least, we cannot be accused of savagery. As for the other matter, see me when you're sober.

JACKSON turns on his heels and stalks off. PAYNE watches

him go.

PAYNE   Ah, well... at least we'll shoot one of the bastards.

He goes off. EGAN, GLEESON, OLIVER, HYNES, and FITZGERALD enter forming a group away from the position of Daly's cell towards which they glance from time to time.

EGAN   I tell youse I've thought about it and thought about it and I don't know. Now why do you suppose they did it?

FITZGERALD   Nobody knows the whys and wherefores of it but I'll tell you the truth will I? I for one am bloody glad of it.

They all nod in agreement.

It's not so easy to sleep when you lie there at night thinking of what it must be like.

EGAN   Like visiting the dentist only worse. At least you come away from the dentist.

OLIVER   Do you think they've gone soft-hearted?

GLEESON   Soft- hearted! The English! Soft- hearted! Oh, Jesus! Do you call penal servitude for life a bloody bed of roses or something?

OLIVER   Where there's life there's hope so they do say.

EGAN   And there's no women in prison.

OLIVER   So we ought to be thankful for small mercies.

EGAN   That's never merciful. That's torment so it is.

GLEESON   *(Softly)* Dead or in jail what's me ould woman going to do?

EGAN   What am I going to do?

HYNES   *(Brandishing a fist)* If you don't shut up, Eugene Egan, I'll shut you up.

FITZGERALD   Yes, what about Jim? He being the only one left? That must be a terrible thing for him.

HYNES   We didn't ask for our sentences to be commuted. We didn't ask anything of them. Jim knows that.

FITZGERALD   But he's no more to blame than the rest of us. We was all in it.

OLIVER   He was the only one they heard. He was the one who shouted out, gave his name.

FITZGERALD   So do they have to make an example of him?

GLEESON   Maybe they thought how one example would be enough, thirteen too many.

EGAN   I was watching his face, I don't know why, when the commandant was reading out the sentences and, do you know, I don't believe he was even listening? I don't believe he heard a single word.

OLIVER   Maybe he already knew.

FITZGERALD   Maybe he was hoping.

EGAN   Why would a man want to die now?

FITZGERALD   To light a spark maybe.

EGAN   One year hard labour, three years penal servitude, one year hard labour, five years, ten, fifteen. And then, when it comes to us, commuted to penal servitude for life. But not

	for you Jim Daly. Your sentence stands and will be carried out in twenty-one days. Just him, all alone. All of us standing there and just him, all alone.
GLEESON	If Josie Hawes had been there and not in the camp hospital there would be the two of them for sure and that's a fact.
OLIVER	We don't know about that.
GLEESON	Do you think they'll let us see Jim?
Silence.	
EGAN	Well, we'll be leaving this stinking country anyway.
HYNES	And it wasn't even the death of you.
EGAN	It damn near was begad. What? With a bullet through me chest and now in an English prison for the rest of me days and never a woman in sight?
FITZGERALD	You'll be alive at least, be thankful for that.
EGAN	Alive is it? Huh!
FITZGERALD	I'll tell you one thing and this is the truth of it, there's none of us will be getting any sleep this night.
GLEESON	Oh, Jesus!

The men, casting a backward glance towards the cell, all leave, except for FITZGERALD who stands there a moment longer.

FITZGERALD	God bless you, Jim Daly.

Then he too turns and goes. The lights come up in the cell. DALY's confession is over. Again we hear the rattling of keys and the slamming back of a heavy bolt and now we see the ESCORT waiting outside the cell as SMYTH enters. (There were in the original escort ten soldiers: two in front of the prisoner, eight following. but it is necessary only to show an escort).

SMYTH　　　　　Are you ready?

DALY gets to his feet, rubs his knee and then, straightening up, takes from his pocket a green handkerchief which he ties loosely about his throat. Then he turns to SMYTH.

DALY　　　　　Ready.

SMYTH steps forward and pins a white disc on DALY's left breast. Then, from one of the escort, he takes a blindfold. DALY steps back.

　　　　　　　　What's that for?

SMYTH　　　　　Regulations.

DALY　　　　　Stuff the regulations. I don't want it.

SMYTH looks appealingly to BAKER.

BAKER　　　　　Jim.

DALY　　　　　I don't want it.

SMYTH　　　　　And we don't want any trouble. I mean... more than... *(He trails off).*

BAKER　　　　　Don't make it more difficult, Jim.

DALY　　　　　What? If I am going to die, as seems to be the case, I want to see it. It's my death. I want to see it. Who is to deny me seeing it?

BAKER   Jim, put it on.

DALY   No, I tell you! No! I don't want it!

BAKER   Please... for me.

DALY glares at BAKER for a moment then turns his back on SMYTH who steps forward and puts on the blindfold.

SMYTH   Not too tight?

As there is no answer, SMYTH takes DALY by the arm and leads him to the door.

The lights come up on a chair which is weighted down with two half cwts tied to the front legs. To one side there stands a LIEUTENANT and the SERGEANT in charge of the firing party facing the chair. A coil of rope lies beside the chair.

There is the sound of men's voices coming from the cells which overlook the square in which the chair is placed.

MEN   Hail Mary full of grace, the Lord is with Thee, Blessed art Thou among women and blessed is the fruit of Thy womb, Jesus. Holy Mary, Mother of God, pray for us sinners now and at the hour of our death.

The recital continues as BAKER appears from behind the cell followed by two soldiers, then DALY and SMYTH, then the rest of the escort. As they come abreast of the chair...

SMYTH   Escort... Escort... halt. Right turn.

This leaves DALY with his back to the chair and facing the firing party. He puts up his hands and removes the bandage from over his eyes, placing it on the ground and under his foot. The LIEUTENANT looks inquiringly at SMYTH who, almost imperceptibly, shakes his head and orders the escort off.

	Escort... Escort, left turn. By the right, quick march.
DALY	Good morning, men. Is it here it's going to be done?
SERGEANT	Daly, sit in the chair.
DALY	*(Turns to look at the chair, then at the SERGEANT)* No. When I am shot I want to be shot like an Irishman and fall to the ground.
LIEUTENANT	It is an order, Daly. Sit.
DALY	An order? *(He smiles)* No.
BAKER	Jim, will you not make another sacrifice?
DALY	What greater sacrifice can I make than what I am doing?
BAKER	Jim, will you do this for me?
DALY	Father, I will, for you. But don't let them tie me. *(To the firing party)* Ye men don't know my mind. You might think I am afraid to die. I am not. And some day the men in the cells over there may be free and ye might meet them somewhere and say I died a coward. But there's one thing ye'll never be able to say, unless you tell lies, that ye ever put a bullet through Daly's shirt.

He takes off his tunic and singlet, leaving himself in shorts, puttees and boots, and his green kerchief. He sits on the chair, folds his arms, looks up at the firing squad.

	Now I am ready.
LIEUTENANT	Firing party load... aim...

His arm is lifted high, in his hand a white handkerchief. The LIGHTS dim. The hand drops. There is a shattering roar and FATHER BAKER moves in quickly to anoint the body. It is all over.

Note of interest: Daly was hit by thirteen bullets and almost cut in two. There was a wall behind the chair in which were imbedded fragments of flesh and bone which were separately gathered by Hawes and a few others and, in two small boxes, interred with the coffin in Dagshai cemetery.

The only LIGHT now is on the cell wall and, as we hear the strains of The Last Post, the circle of LIGHT gets smaller and smaller until it is focused on the figures "The 88th".

A VOICE is heard reading.

VOICE — Order for Disbandenment, Army Order 78/1922. March 11th. His Majesty the King has approved with great regret the disbandment, as soon as the exigencies of the service permit, the following corps and battalions of Infantry of the Line.

The Royal Irish Fusiliers.

The Connaught Rangers.

The Prince of Wales Leinster Regiment.

The Royal Canadians.

The Royal Munster Fusiliers.

The Royal Dublin Fusiliers.

The light on "The 88th" fades into darkness as THE CURTAIN FALLS.